ORIGINS AND EARLY DEVELOPMENT OF HUMAN BODY KNOWLEDGE

Virginia Slaughter
Michelle Heron

IN COLLABORATION WITH
Linda Jenkins
Elizabeth Tilse

WITH COMMENTARY BY
Ulrich Müller
Dana Liebermann

Willis F. Overton
Series Editor

 **Blackwell**
Publishing   *Boston, Massachusetts   Oxford, United Kingdom*

ORIGINS AND EARLY DEVELOPMENT OF HUMAN BODY KNOWLEDGE

CONTENTS

COMMENTARY

ABSTRACT

As a knowable object, the human body is highly complex. Evidence from several converging lines of research, including psychological studies, neuroimaging and clinical neuropsychology, indicates that human body knowledge is widely distributed in the adult brain, and is instantiated in at least three partially independent levels of representation. Sensori-motor body knowledge is responsible for on-line control and movement of one's own body and may also contribute to the perception of others' moving bodies; visuo-spatial body knowledge specifies detailed structural descriptions of the spatial attributes of the human body; and lexical–semantic body knowledge contains language-based knowledge about the human body. In the first chapter of this *Monograph*, we outline the evidence for these three hypothesized levels of human body knowledge, then review relevant literature on infants' and young children's human body knowledge in terms of the three-level framework. In Chapters II and III, we report two complimentary series of studies that specifically investigate the emergence of visuo-spatial body knowledge in infancy. Our technique is to compare infants' responses to typical and scrambled human bodies, in order to evaluate when and how infants acquire knowledge about the canonical spatial layout of the human body. Data from a series of visual habituation studies indicate that infants first discriminate scrambled from typical human body pictures at 15 to 18 months of age. Data from object examination studies similarly indicate that infants are sensitive to violations of three-dimensional human body stimuli starting at 15–18 months of age. The overall pattern of data supports several conclusions about the early development of human body knowledge: (a) detailed visuo-spatial knowledge about the human body is first evident in the second year of life, (b) visuo-spatial knowledge of human faces and human bodies are at least partially independent in infancy and (c) infants' initial visuo-spatial human body representations appear to be highly schematic, becoming more detailed and specific with development. In the final chapter, we explore these conclusions and discuss how levels of body knowledge may interact in early development.

I. LEVELS OF HUMAN BODY KNOWLEDGE IN DEVELOPMENT

When adults look at the images presented in Figure 1, we recognize that some of them (namely, those in the lower row) are strange looking, impossible human figures. This realization is fairly effortless and we can easily classify some of the images as belonging to the category of typical human body shapes whereas others belong to a category of atypical or impossible human body shapes. Presumably, these judgements are made with reference to a mental representation—a template, image or concept—of the structure of the human body that we all share. This representation engenders recognition of the body as a physical object, and specifies its typical shape and the arrangement of parts in the whole. The questions this *Monograph* addresses are: At what age do infants discriminate different human body shapes, and what does the development of this ability tell us about the origins and early development of knowledge about the human body?

THE "BODY SCHEMA"

It has long been suggested that the human body occupies a special place in both the adult and developing mind. There are a number of facets to this assumption. Human cognition is "embodied" in the sense that the experiences that inform our knowledge are constrained by the sensory and motor functions that the body makes (Johnson, 1987; Lakoff, 1987; Overton, 1994; Thelen, 1995b; Varela, Thompson, & Rosch, 1991). The human body is special because it, unlike any other object, is known from both the inside and from without, from first- and third-person perspectives. The body is not only a knowable object in its own right, but it also serves as a vehicle for conveying information about other individuals, including their transient mental states such as direction of attention and emotion, personal identity specified by an individual's characteristic body postures and movement patterns, and aspects of social identity such as gender, age and attractiveness. The human body is therefore highly complex and occupies a unique

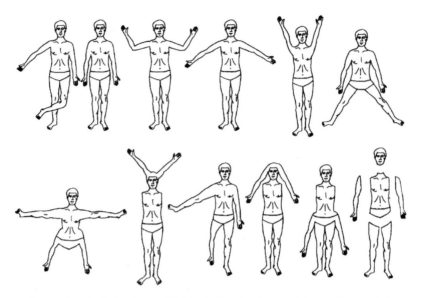

FIGURE 1.—Typical and scrambled body line drawings used in Studies 1 and 2.

place in the world of knowable physical objects, and on that basis it has been suggested that the body is subject to dedicated cognitive representations and processes. Empirically, this assumption is supported by cognitive and neuropsychological studies, mainly with adult participants, that have shown that human body knowledge can be isolated from other domains of knowledge.

For the last century, investigators have noted that some types of brain damage can result in symptoms that implicate a disruption in some aspect of an individual's knowledge about the human body (see Denes, 1989; Goldenberg, 1997; Poeck & Orgass, 1971 for reviews). These sorts of syndromes came to be known as disorders of the "body schema." However, the syndromes that were together classified as disorders of the body schema were highly variable with respect to the breadth and explicitness of knowledge about the body that was thought to be disturbed, for instance hemi-neglect, in which patients ignore one side of their bodies, and body part anomia, in which patients are incapable of correctly naming parts of the body, were both classified as body schema disturbances, despite their being defined by very different types of symptoms (perceptual-motor dysfunction on the one hand, and a form of aphasia on the other). As a number of authors have noted, the only thing that unifies these disorders is their having something to do with the body; the underlying representations and cognitive functions that are disturbed in these disparate "disorders of the body schema" may well be distinct (Denes, 1989; Poeck & Orgass, 1971; Reed, 2002).

2

The idea that the human body is subject to unique or dedicated mental representations is compelling, and so the term "body schema" has been adopted by a number of authors. Unfortunately there has been no consensus regarding a single definition for the term. The body schema has been conceptualized as anything from first person bodily awareness, to any kind of conceptual knowledge about the structure or functioning of human bodies in general. To further complicate matters, there is also a history of terminological inconsistency, with "body schema" and "body image" being used interchangeably by some authors, and other terms, including body percept, body template, body map, and somatopsyche also used to refer to knowledge about the body (Elian, Marcel, & Bermudez, 1995; Gallagher, 2004; Poeck & Orgass, 1971; Reed, 2002).

LEVELS OF HUMAN BODY KNOWLEDGE: A COGNITIVE NEUROPSYCHOLOGICAL PERSPECTIVE

Recently, a number of authors have sought to clarify the confusion by defining different levels of body knowledge (Sirigu, Grafman, Bressler, & Sunderland, 1991). In this context, the term "levels" of body knowledge is used in recognition of the fact that human body knowledge is complex and multi-faceted, and is likely to be instantiated in more than one neural system. Theoretically, it is clear that human body knowledge includes a number of different levels, from direct sensori-motor knowledge of one's own body all the way up to factual knowledge about the human body as a biological organism. Empirically, distinctions among levels of human body knowledge are based on what is known about how the body is represented in the brain, and also on behavioral evidence from perceptual and cognitive tasks that reveal dissociations in aspects of body knowledge, often in individuals who have suffered brain damage. These perspectives reveal three distinct levels, types, or systems of human body knowledge in adults, distinguished by the durability of the underlying representations, their cognitive function, and accessibility to consciousness.

An important distinction in the literature on levels of human body knowledge is between short-term, sensori-motor representations of one's own body, versus long-term representations that support knowledge about bodies in general (including one's own). Recent neuropsychological studies have revealed that a number of interacting brain areas contribute to the representation of one's own body; these include sensory cortex, premotor and primary motor cortex and the parietal lobes (see Graziano & Botvinick, 2002 for a review). Some of these areas also contribute to the perception and interpretation of others' bodily motion (Gallese, Fadiga, Fogassi, &

Rizzolatti, 2002; Shiffrar & Pinto, 2002). The consensus is that this level of human body knowledge is specifically short-term, dynamic and first-person, responsible for sensori-motor activity and basic awareness of one's own body (Goldenberg, 1997; Reed, 2002), and not accessible to conscious reflection (Gallagher, 1995; 2004). Evidence for the existence of this level of human body knowledge as distinct from other types of body knowledge comes from clinical syndromes that implicate specific deficits in aspects of one's own sensori-motor performance and/or awareness. These include hemi-neglect, in which patients do not register sensori-motor input or output for one half of their bodies, optic apraxia in which patients are unable to perform visually guided reaches, and phantom limbs, in which patients experience sensation in missing limbs. It is important to note that patients with these sensori-motor disorders typically do not realize that their body knowledge is erroneous; this supports the idea that this level of knowledge about the body is implicit (Gallagher, 2004). As Gallagher, Butterworth, Lew, and Cole (1998) note, the existence of several cases of phantom limbs in children with congenital limb deletions suggests that at least some elements of this level of body representation are likely to be instantiated in built-in, species-specific neuro-motor circuitry.

In addition to sensori-motor representations of the body, we have all sorts of knowledge about bodies in general. This type of knowledge about the body is characterized by long-term representations that are accessible to conscious reflection (Gallagher, 1995; 2004; Reed, 2002). Recent case studies of patients with parietal lobe brain damage indicate further that long-term representations of the human body comprise two distinct levels: a visuo-spatial level that specifies the topological features of the whole body, its parts and how they relate to each other in the whole, and a lexical–semantic level that involves language-based knowledge about the body (Goldenberg, 1997; Sirigu et al., 1991).

Evidence for distinct visuo-spatial representations of the human body derives from the clinical syndrome known as autotopagnosia. Patients with this disorder have a specific deficit in that they cannot find specific body parts when asked to point them out. When invited to "point to your shoulder", autotopagnosic patients fumble around, often pointing to a nearby body part (e.g., elbow instead of shoulder) and remarking that they can't find it, or "it's around here somewhere" (Ogden, 1985; Guariglia, Piccardi, Puglisi Allegra, & Traballesi, 2002; Semenza, 1988). The deficit in body part localization applies whether the target part is on their own body, on another person's body or on representations of bodies including photographs, mannequins and dolls (but see Felician, Ceccaldi, Didic, Thinus-Blanc, & Poncet, 2003 for an autotopagnosic individual who showed a self-only body part localization deficit). The deficit also extends to other spatial tasks including matching identical body postures across different views (Denes,

4

Cappelletti, Zilli, Dalla Porta, & Gallana, 2000) and verbally describing the location of body parts (Ogden, 1985; DeRenzi & Scotti, 1970; but see Guariglia et al., 2002). Control tasks show that the autotopagnosic deficit in body part localization is specific to human bodies as the majority of patients can localize parts of other complex objects (bicycles) and in some cases, body parts of animals (Semenza, 1988; Guariglia et al., 2002; but see DeRenzi & Scotti, 1970).

The majority of patients with autotopagnosia exhibit normal everyday behavior, indicating that their sensori-motor body representations are intact. These patients also tend to perform well on nonlocalization tasks indicating that lexical–semantic knowledge of the human body is intact. For instance, most autotopagnosic patients who fail to localize body parts can nevertheless name body parts when those parts are presented in pictures or touched on their own bodies (Buxbaum & Coslett, 2001; Ogden, 1985; Sirigu et al., 1991); they can name parts of clothing associated with specific body parts (sleeves, hats) in spite of failing to localize the related body parts (Ogden, 1985; Buxbaum & Coslett, 2001); and they can describe the functions of body parts (e.g., eyes are for seeing; Guariglia et al., 2002; Sirigu et al., 1991). Further evidence for a dissociable level of lexical–semantic human body knowledge comes from case studies of a different clinical syndrome, body part anomia, in which patients exhibit specific problems with body part naming (Dennis, 1976; Coslett, Saffran, & Schwoebel, 2002). The fact that these different syndromes exist independently, and usually result from brain damage in different (though often adjacent) locations in the left parietal lobe, suggests that the representations underlying visuo-spatial and lexical–semantic knowledge of the human body are at least partially independent. Patients with disorders that implicate disturbances in visuo-spatial or lexical–semantic body knowledge are often aware that their body knowledge is erroneous, indicating that these levels of knowledge, unlike the sensori-motor level, are accessible to consciousness.

This brief review reveals three levels of partially-independent human body representations in adults: sensori-motor representations that are implicit and responsible for on-line bodily control and movement, visuo-spatial representations that contain general structural descriptions of the spatial attributes of the body and its parts, and lexical–semantic representations that entail propositional knowledge about the body including the names of parts and their functions, semantic associations, and so on.

Now we turn to the investigation of when and how these levels of body knowledge emerge during development. Buxbaum and Coslett (2001) hint at a possible developmental trajectory when they propose that visuo-spatial and lexical–semantic body knowledge are derived from the more basic sensori-motor body knowledge. This idea is not new; classic authors also suggested that the motor/postural body representations evident in an

5

infant's behavior could be foundational for later-developing body knowledge (see Piaget, 1953; Poeck & Orgass, 1971). We return to this proposal in later chapters.

DEVELOPMENTAL LEVELS OF REPRESENTATION

The foregoing review outlined three levels of human body knowledge derived from empirical work with adults. These partially independent levels of body knowledge are hypothesized to entail distinct "levels" of representation: sensori-motor, visuo-spatial, and lexical–semantic. In the remainder of this chapter, we review what is known about the early development of human body knowledge, and organize the review with respect to those three levels of body knowledge. In order to avoid historically confusing terminology (e.g., body schema, body image, etc.) we refer to these levels of body knowledge with terms that are descriptive of the nature of the underlying representations: sensori-motor body knowledge, visuo-spatial body knowledge, and lexical–semantic body knowledge. In line with this terminology, we adopt a minimal definition for representation as simply any type of "stored knowledge" (Mandler, 1998) about the body within these three different levels.[1]

The "levels" of body knowledge outlined above are defined essentially by content (e.g., the type of stored knowledge about the body, and the behavioral and cognitive functions that knowledge allows). We acknowledge that these "levels" are not necessarily consistent with developmental perspectives on levels of knowledge. According to classic developmental theory (e.g., Piaget, 1953), knowledge structures develop progressively through a series of levels, from sensori-motor action schemes, to mental representation, to symbolic representations (see Karmiloff-Smith, 1992; Müller, Sokol, & Overton, 1998 for updated versions of this perspective). Within the framework for human body knowledge derived from empirical and theoretical analyses of the structure of adults' body knowledge, each "level" of body knowledge (e.g., sensori-motor, visuo-spatial, lexical–semantic) may involve representations at different developmental levels of complexity. For instance, as we discuss below, some forms of neonatal behavior implicate sensori-motor body representations because they reflect stored knowledge about the body that allows for implicit, on-line bodily control; however, these behaviors do not necessarily imply representational knowledge at a more complex level than that of sensori-motor action schemes. In the following review we discuss evidence for developing body knowledge with respect to the three-level framework introduced above, and also attempt to clarify how the evidence relates to developmental levels of representation.

6

EVIDENCE FOR SENSORI-MOTOR BODY KNOWLEDGE IN INFANCY

Intermodal Coordination

Neonates have more control over their bodies than was once thought, and this capacity for simple bodily coordinations may constitute at least the beginnings of sensori-motor body knowledge. In particular, there is evidence that newborns coordinate inputs from their different senses, and control their motor behavior accordingly. Some examples of sensori-motor coordination are seen in the newborn reflexes: neonates will turn their heads in the direction of a sound and they will make defensive arm and head movements to remove a felt object from the face (Brazelton, Nugent, & Lester, 1987). In addition to coordinated reflex behaviors, newborns also exhibit coordinated hand-to-mouth movements in which the mouth opens in anticipation of the hand's arrival (Butterworth & Hopkins, 1988) and object-driven pre-reaching gestures that reveal coordination of arm and hand movement with visual input (von Hofsten, 1982; Ronnqvist & von Hofsten, 1994). These newborn skills indicate that sensory and motor systems are at least partially integrated at birth, and that type of basic bodily integration implicates the sensori-motor level of body knowledge, thought to be responsible for on-line bodily control. Such congenital coordinations do not necessarily implicate mental representations (but see Meltzoff & Borton, 1979; Meltzoff, Kuhl & Moore, 1991); instead they may simply exist as a function of built-in neuro-motor circuitry, and those inbuilt structures may be foundational for later development of sensori-motor representations.

A number of visual preference studies have specifically examined infants' knowledge of their own bodies by providing opportunities for kinaesthetic-visual matching. By three to five months of age, infants show coordination of their own felt and viewed movements reflected in the fact that they look reliably longer at video images of the moving legs of same-aged peers, compared with on-line images of their own legs (Bahrick & Watson, 1985; Rochat & Morgan, 1995; Schmuckler, 1996). This pattern of looking demonstrates a capacity not just to coordinate visual information and motor behavior, but also suggests that infants are integrating sensory and motor information from their own bodies into a coherent representation, in order to compare images of self and other. Some authors propose that this capacity to integrate different elements of one's own bodily experience is the foundation of a sense of self (Neisser, 1988; Rochat, 1995; Stern, 1985).

Rochat and Morgan (1995) found that 3–5-month-old infants discriminated video images that portrayed an incongruent view of their own legs (meaning that each leg image was reversed so that it appeared to move in the opposite direction to the felt direction of leg movement) from a congruent view, suggesting that infants not only match contingency information (I feel movement–I see movement) but that they match details of the felt and seen movement (I move right–I see rightward movement). Schmuckler (1996) replicated this pattern with infants viewing their own hands in congruent and incongruent views.

Morgan and Rochat (1997) further showed that 5-month-old infants visually discriminated images that portrayed their moving legs in a standard view, versus their legs in a reversed view whereby the left leg was shown to the right of midline and the right leg was shown to the left. When puffy leggings were put on the infants so that the features of their legs were obscured, infants no longer discriminated the two views. These authors argued that by five months of age, infants have some expectations about the appearance of their own bodies, namely expectations about the biomechanical features of their legs (see also Schmuckler & Fairhall, 2001). According to Rochat and colleagues, these findings indicate that infants have access to a representation of the invariant structure of their own bodies (that they term a "body schema"; Rochat, 1998; Morgan & Rochat, 1997). Thus within the first 6 months of life, sensori-motor body knowledge may develop from the simple bodily coordinations evident at birth, to involve more flexible, dynamic representations of the infant's own body.

Neonatal Imitation

The phenomenon of neonatal imitation, if real, can also suggest that infants possess sensori-motor representations of their own bodies, and further, it supports the idea that this level of body knowledge can also be recruited in the perception and interpretation of others' bodies.

Meltzoff and Moore (1977, 1983, 1989) reported that newborns as young as several minutes old copied the gestures of adult models; these included mouth opening, tongue protrusion and lip protrusion. In one study, they also reported imitation of sequential finger movements by neonates (Meltzoff & Moore, 1977). This finding was initially controversial because it challenged long-held Piagetian beliefs about the cognitive capabilities of infants. The main issue was whether newborns have a capacity for mental representation: According to Meltzoff and Moore (1977, 1983), if newborns imitate facial gestures, that implicates a representational system that relates visually perceived motor movements to proprioceptively generated ones. This analysis of neonatal imitation continues to be controversial. Further controversy has arisen because of problems replicating the basic phenomenon.

Over the last two decades, numerous researchers have attempted replications of Meltzoff and Moore's findings. Some of these replications have been successful and have even extended the range of facial gestures that newborns will imitate (Field, Woodson, Greenberg, & Cohen, 1982; Legerstee, 1991; see Meltzoff & Moore, 1997 for a review). However, other researchers have been unable to replicate the basic finding, and some have found that only a limited number of behaviors are imitated by newborns, perhaps reflexively (Abranvel & Sigafoos, 1984; see Anisfeld, 1991, 1996 for reviews; Jones, 1996). There are also reports of neonatal "imitation" of nonhuman models (Jacobson, 1979, but see Legerstee, 1991).

Even if newborns only imitate tongue protrusion (Anisfeld, 1996), the phenomenon implicates some rudimentary sensori-motor body knowledge at the level of basic bodily coordination, like that discussed in the previous section. However, as Meltzoff and Moore have argued, if newborns are capable of flexibly imitating a range of different gestures, that implies that neonates have a capacity to map visual information about human body movement of another to proprioceptive information about body movement of the self. The hypothesis is that this mapping is achieved by a "supramodal" body representation that codes for bodily movement in general such that 'perceived other' is equivalent to 'felt own' (Meltzoff & Moore, 1995, 1997; see also Gallagher & Meltzoff, 1996; Meltzoff & Gopnik, 1993).

Recent work in the neurosciences provides some evidence for the existence of a gestural mirroring system in human adults, that could operate as a supramodal representational system like that hypothesized by Meltzoff and Moore. This system is thought to be similar to the individual "mirror" neurons recently discovered in the monkey premotor cortex, which fire both when actions are performed by the self and when the same actions are seen to be performed by others (Carey, 1996; Gallese, Fadiga, Fogassi, & Rizzolatti, 1996). In adult humans, brain imaging studies show that the same regions that are active when an individual performs specific motor movements also respond when another person is observed performing those movements (see Gallese et al., 2002 for a review). As mentioned above, this suggests that in adults, sensori-motor body representations participate in both performance and perception of bodily movement. A recent EEG study suggests that the same is true of preschool-aged children (Martineau & Cochin, 2003). Whether the same is true in infancy requires further study. However, it is notable in this context that newborns only imitate if they see the dynamics of a gesture; just seeing the end state (e.g., a tongue poking out) is not sufficient to elicit imitation until late in the first year (Vinter, 1986). Thus neonatal imitation may rely on dynamic, movement-based representations, characteristic of the sensori-motor level of body knowledge.

The previous section reviewed the evidence that sensori-motor representations of the body code for dynamic gestures, both performed and perceived. However, infants also demonstrate sensitivity to human movements that they are not yet fully capable of performing (Shiffrar & Pinto, 2002). Evidence for this comes from infants' responses to "point-light displays" (PLDs) of human walkers. To create PLDs, actors are filmed walking around in the dark while wearing black suits with light-reflecting patches affixed to the major joints (e.g., wrist, elbows, etc.). The resulting films reveal a dozen or so luminous dots moving across a dark field, producing in adults a compelling percept of a coherent human figure in motion (Johansson, 1973). Research with adults has shown that observers can readily perceive complex features of such displays, including details of gait (marching vs. walking), specific actions (pushing vs. pulling), emotions (surprise vs. fear) and other features (see Shiffrar, 2001 and Thorton, Pinto, & Shiffrar, 1998 for reviews). Perception of human movement from PLDs is fast, effortless and independent of IQ, as demonstrated in studies with in various clinical groups (Moore, Hobson, & Anderson, 1995; Moore, Hobson, & Lee, 1997).

To test whether infants perceive PLDs as portraying human movement, as adults do, researchers have simultaneously presented infants with PLDs of different movement patterns, and measured their looking preferences. Several studies using this methodology have shown that infants between the ages of three and six months look longer at a PLD walker compared to control displays, including incoherent displays generated by transposing the locations of the dots, inverting PLD walkers or presenting out-of-phase dot movement (Bertenthal, Proffitt, & Cutting, 1984; Bertenthal, Proffitt, Kramer, & Spetner, 1987; Fox & McDaniel, 1982). In these studies, young infants preferred to look at the PLD displays that represented true human figures, walking upright. If sensori-motor body representations code for both perceived and executed actions, this leads to the question of how pre-walking infants interpret these displays. Bertenthal (1993) found that when 3-, 5- and 7-month-olds were presented with a PLD walker and an out-of-phase pattern of dots, all infants preferred the PLD walker to the altered dots when they were presented upright, but only the 3-month-olds preferred the PLD walker when the displays were inverted. Thus after 3 months of age, infants showed a preference for human movement only if it was presented in the canonical, upright orientation. To explain this pattern of results, Bertenthal (1993) proposed that 3-month-old infants are sensitive to the relational qualities of human biomechanical motion inherent in both upright and inverted walker displays, without actually perceiving the upright walker as a human in motion. Older infants, in contrast, may perceive the upright PLD walker display as a familiar pattern, interpreting it in terms of "stored knowledge about the human form" (Bertenthal, 1993, p. 208). This stored knowledge could be in the form of sensori-motor body representations, derived from infants' own motor experience, their perceptual experiences, or both. If the same body representations are relevant to action and perception (Gallese et al., 2002), then the early motor experience of infants, which includes alternate leg kicking that is motorically identical to walking (Thelen, 1995b; Shiffrar & Pinto, 2002), might contribute to sensori-motor representations that influence older infants' perception of PLD displays as moving human bodies.

In this section, we have reviewed evidence for sensori-motor body knowledge in infancy. This level of body knowledge is characterized by implicit, short-term representations that support on-line bodily movement and control. Thus sensori-motor body knowledge in infancy may include the intermodal coordinations evident in early infancy, as well as dynamic representations hypothesized to underlie neonatal imitation. Older infants' capacity for self/nonself discriminations and perception of PLD walkers provides further evidence for sensori-motor representations in infancy, and these may be involved in the perception of others' bodily movements as well as on-line control of one's own body. These representations presumably become increasingly complex and flexible as infants' motor control and skill develop, though according to the cognitive neuropsychological model, they remain implicit, dynamic and relatively short-term. Detailed studies of motor development support that hypothesis; at least in childhood, sensori-motor representations responsible for control and movement of one's own body are always constrained by the immediate organism–environment interaction (Adolph, 1997, 2000). Later in development, children acquire knowledge about their own motor skills, but this knowledge, both from the cognitive neuropsychological and developmental perspectives, would be instantiated not at the sensori-motor level, but rather in symbolic, lexical–semantic body representations.

EVIDENCE FOR VISUO-SPATIAL BODY KNOWLEDGE IN INFANCY

As noted above, in adults, sensori-motor human body knowledge may interact with, but is dissociable from, visuo-spatial and lexical–semantic body knowledge. Next, we review evidence for the visuo-spatial level of body knowledge in infancy. The question here is: when does a representation of the topological features of bodies in general, emerge in development?

Face Recognition

One of the first experimental studies with infants showed that infants prefer to look at human facial patterns compared to other patterns (Fantz, 1963). This finding set off a wave of research investigating various aspects of face recognition in infancy. It is now well established that within the first few months of life, infants show a strong preference for stimuli that resemble human faces over comparably complex, high-contrast patterns (see Maurer, 1985 for a review). Further, even newborns show a preference for human facial stimuli, evidenced in their tendency to visually track faces (Johnson, Dziurawiec, Ellis, & Morton, 1991). Studies investigating the source of infants' preference for faces have demonstrated that it is the specific configuration of faces that gets infants' attention: They prefer typical human faces in comparison with face patterns in which the constituent features have been scrambled, or a head shape with no internal features (Goren, Sarty, & Wu, 1975; Johnson et al., 1991). The method of comparing infants' responses to typical and scrambled faces controls for the possibility that infants are attracted to displays that contain the parts of faces (e.g., eyes, mouth, nose), without having a preference for how those parts are assembled. The fact that infants demonstrate preferences for typical, as opposed to scrambled, face patterns indicates that infants have very specific early expectations about the spatial properties of human faces.

Studies building on the finding that infants prefer faces show that infants learn rapidly about faces in the weeks after birth, enabling specific discriminations within the domain of faces. For instance, within the first several days of life, newborns prefer the individual faces of their mothers to those of strangers (Field, Cohen, Garcia, & Greenberg, 1984). In terms of categorical discriminations, newborns can differentiate between happy, sad, and surprised facial expressions (Field, Woodson, Greenberg, & Cohen, 1982; Nelson, 1987) and prefer adult-rated attractive to unattractive female faces (Langlois, Roggman, Casey, Ritter, Rieser-Danner, & Jenkins, 1987; Slater, Von der Schulenburg, Brown, Badenoch, Butterworth, Parsons, & Samuels, 1998).

It is not entirely clear how infants pick out human faces as preferred visual stimuli. According to one model, the Conspec/Conlern model (Johnson & Morton, 1991; Johnson, 1997), infants are born with a template, or representation of the human face that directs early attention to, and drives the early preference for facial stimuli. According to this model, the inborn face template is a highly schematic facial pattern, consisting of three high-contrast blobs in a bounded region, spatially corresponding to the two eyes and mouth on a human face. Newborns preferentially track such three-blob stimuli, as well as more specified facial patterns (e.g., patterns containing detailed eyes, nose, and mouth). According to the Conspec model newborn tracking of facial stimuli is an innate, automatic behavior, driven by sub-cortical mechanisms, that biases infants' visual attention towards faces and thereby ensures that they learn about faces in early infancy. Within two months after birth, cortical processes (labeled Conlern in the model) are hypothesized to take over, overriding the innate preference for highly schematic faces, but building on the early learning and directing infants' attention to realistic human face stimuli. Thus the Conspec/Conlern model proposes that newborns pick out human faces by virtue of an innate, schematic representation of the human face that directs attention to human faces, and guides subsequent learning about faces, eventually giving way to higher-level (cortical) face processing.

An alternate, nonrepresentational account for newborns' face preferences is that the neonatal visual system is tuned to recognize, track, and fixate face-like patterns. According to this model, infants are born not with a schematic three-blob template that matches the human face, but with general perceptual biases to attend to and prefer any patterns, facial or nonfacial, that have relatively high contrast at the top of a bounded region (Turati, Simion, Milani, & Umilta, 2002; Valenza, Simion, Macchi Cassia, & Umilta, 1996). This model proposes that the basis of infants' face preferences is a nonspecific perceptual bias, rather than an innate face template; however, in the newborn's natural environment, human faces are the most likely objects that conform to such a pattern, so a bounded region with high contrast on top may be functionally equivalent to an innate representation of a face. On either model, the earliest form of knowledge about human faces is highly schematic, becoming more detailed and specific with development. This implies that at least one element of visuo-spatial body knowledge—knowledge about the face—is present at birth, albeit in a highly schematic form.

Is the face somehow special, or does the early face preference imply that infants also have visuo-spatial knowledge about the rest of the human form? It has been suggested that the face is indeed a 'special' visual object, handled by unique and dedicated object recognition mechanisms in the brain (Kanwisher, McDermott, & Chun, 1997; but see Tanaka & Gauthier, 1997). The issue of whether the body is a similarly 'special' object is open to debate (see Slaughter, Stone, & Reed, in press). It is worth noting here that autotopagnosics tested on face recognition show some deficits in the visual processing of faces; when presented with a face puzzle and asked to put the internal parts in the correct configuration, autotopagnosic patients failed by making mistakes like exchanging eyes for ears, and inverting the mouth (Guariglia et al., 2002; Ogden, 1985). These data support the idea that the face is part of the overall body representation, such that localized brain damage can cause concurrent disruption of face and body visuo-spatial processing. However, it should also be noted that autotopagnosics typically

13

do not suffer prosopagnosia, the inability to recognize individual faces, which indicates that some aspects of their face processing are intact, and further indicates some dissociation in face and body visual representations. We return to this issue of similarities and differences in the recognition of face and body configurations below.

Categorization of Humans

Categorization studies aimed at investigating infants' ability to discriminate humans from other complex stimuli provide indirect information about infants' human body knowledge. As these studies present pictures and toy models to infants, they test infants' responses to the structural layout of the human body, and therefore tap visuo-spatial human body knowledge.

Quinn and Eimas (1998; Quinn, 2002) investigated young infants' categorization of pictures of humans and nonhuman mammals. They familiarized 3–4-month old infants with pictures of adults (presented in pairs), in which each picture displayed a different person, in a different position, wearing different clothes. In a second condition, the infants were similarly familiarized to pictures of various animals. During the test-phase, infants saw new pairs of pictures showing one previously unseen exemplar of the familiar category, paired with a new exemplar of a contrasting category, taken from both the animate and inanimate domains. When infants were familiarized with humans, they showed no preference for any of the out-of-category exemplars from the animate domain (cat, dog, horse). Such a preference only occurred for an inanimate object (e.g., a car). However, when pictures of either horses or cats were used for familiarization, infants preferred to look at the exemplar of a contrasting category, whether it was a different animal, a human, or a car. This pattern of results indicates that different processes underlie infants' categorization of humans and other animals.

To explain this asymmetry in categorization of humans versus animals, Quinn and Eimas (1998) suggest that infants' knowledge of human beings is both richer and broader than that of other animals, and this affects their categorizations. Because infants are likely to have experience with a number of individual humans, but relatively few animals, they suggest that in the first few months of life infants rapidly become "experts" at categorizing humans. Infants may come into the experimental procedure with experience of humans that includes familiarity with many specific exemplars (individual humans) as well as a summary representation, or prototype derived from that experience. This prototype would be an established representation of humans that includes visuo-spatial information about the human body. In contrast to their rich history of experience of humans, Quinn and Eimas argue that young infants are likely to have relatively limited experience with animals, and therefore are unlikely to come into the experimental procedure with established knowledge about animals. Thus when presented with an animal picture following familiarization with humans, infants may perceive the animal as being similar to the human prototype (primed in the familiarization phase), and therefore treat the animal as a member of the human category. Thus the early asymmetry in categorization of humans versus animals is explained in terms of differential experience with the categories.

Quinn and Eimas suggest that infants' willingness to accept animals into the category of human beings indicates that developmentally, humans serve as a cognitive "reference point" for categorization of animals in general. They further propose that the human body structure of a prominent face/head and an elongated body with appendages is the basis for infants' perception of similarity between animals and humans, and this body structure may provide a basic template for animals in general, with humans as the "best" example of the category. In Quinn and Eimas' view (1998), this template is a schematic mental representation of the structure of the human body, reminiscent of the proposed schematic quality of infants' early knowledge of the face.

To directly explore the importance of body shape in the categorization of humans and animals, Quinn (2002) tested 3- and 4-month-old infants' categorization of humans and animals by contrasting conditions in which the stimuli were pictures of heads only, bodies only, and whole bodies. Quinn (2002) replicated the asymmetry in infants' categorization of humans versus cats, only if whole-body information was presented; it was not enough to show human heads or bodies alone. Thus infants included cats in their human category only if the humans were presented from head to toe. Interestingly, this is in contrast to the pattern obtained when animals alone were presented for categorization; cats and dogs were successfully categorized by young infants on the basis of head information alone (Quinn & Eimas, 1996).

Pauen (2000) ran a similar study exploring infants' categorization of humans versus animals and found that by seven months of age, infants dishabituated to an animal following familiarization with humans. Comparing this finding with Quinn and Eimas (1998) suggests the conclusion that infants' categorization of at least some animals diverges from the hypothesized human "reference point" by the age of 7 months. Pauen (2000) also concluded that humans are represented as a category distinct from other mammals by 7 months of age. According to Quinn and Eimas' developmental model, this change may reflects infants' increasing familiarity with animals, leading to summary representations of animals that help infants identify them as being dissimilar to humans.

15

Other methods that have been used to explore infants' categorization of humans reveal later developmental trends. For instance, Ross (1980) found evidence for categorization of humans and animals only at 12 months with an object examination task, in which infants were allowed to handle and examine three-dimensional models depicting members of one ontological category (e.g., humans, animals, vehicles), and then they were presented with an exemplar from a contrasting category. Recovery of interest, or extended examination of the contrasting exemplar, is taken as evidence for categorization in this paradigm. Pauen (2000) replicated Ross's study with younger infants, and established that 7-, 9-, and 11-month-old infants distinguished humans from mammals with this methodology. Oakes, Plumert, Lasink, and Merryman (1996) conducted two experiments comparing 10- and 13-month-old infants' discrimination of humans versus animals in object-examination and sequential-touching tasks. Using an object-examination task, both age groups distinguished between animals and humans. When infants were tested using a sequential touching task (requiring sequential handling of items from a single category) only 13-month-old infants distinguished between the two categories. These results highlight a point made by Oakes and colleagues (1996) and others (Mareschal & Quinn, 2001; Ross, 1980; Younger & Furrer, 2003), namely, that conclusions about infants' categorization abilities cannot necessarily be made independently of the methodology employed, the response measured, the categories presented, and the input history in a given experimental paradigm.

Mandler (1997, 2000) has argued that visual and manual tasks tap two distinct categorization processes in infancy. Mandler proposes that visual tasks reflect perceptual categorization processes that are based on surface properties like shape and texture. Manual tasks on the other hand reflect conceptual categorization processes that are based on relatively more complex object properties such as movement, behavior and agent–patient relationship roles. If correct, this would suggest that something more than visuo-spatial categorization of the human form is necessary for infants to discriminate humans from animals on the manual tasks described above. We address this controversial proposal (see Quinn & Eimas, 2000; Quinn, Johnson, Mareschal, Rakison, & Younger, 2000, for discussions) in the studies reported below by comparing infants' performance across visual and manual human body categorization tasks.

In sum, the infant categorization work indicates that by four months of age infants discriminate humans from other animals (but not vice versa) on the basis of body shape. Exhaustive categorization of humans versus animals has been demonstrated in different categorization paradigms by around the end of the first year of life. Quinn and Eimas (1996) suggest that the early discrimination of humans from animals is based on knowledge about the typical human form, schematically represented by facial attributes and an elongated body with appendages. If this is the case, when does that early, schematic knowledge of the human form develop into the detailed visuo-spatial body knowledge evident in adults?

Infants' Preferences for Typical Versus Scrambled Human Body Pictures

We earlier tested the question of when infants acquire detailed visuo-spatial human body knowledge by exploring when infants discriminated typical human body shapes from atypical or scrambled human body shapes (Slaughter, Heron, & Sim, 2002). Following the logic of the face recognition research, we created scrambled human body pictures that were equated with typical body pictures for amount of contour and contrast, but violated the canonical human body structure. The six typical body pictures showed a human standing in a variety of postures, and the six scrambled body pictures showed violations of the typical human body shape, constructed by moving the limbs to noncanonical locations on the body (see Figure 1). Bodies were scrambled according to the following logic: the head, torso, arms, and legs were identified as basic-level body parts (Johnson & Kendrick, 1984) whose names are learned relatively early (Witt, Cermack, & Coster, 1990; see discussion below), so these were the units that were manipulated to create scrambled bodies. Scrambling involved moving the arms and legs to noncannonical locations while maintaining symmetry of the overall pattern (because infants are sensitive to changes in symmetry alone; Bornstein & Krinsky, 1985). The head remained at the top of the scrambled body patterns because we wanted to assess infants' specific knowledge about the structure of the human body and pilot work suggested that bodies with heads moved from the top are confusing with respect to whether they are human at all.

A design comparing infants' responses to typical and scrambled bodies was chosen for two reasons: (a) because such a design controls for the possibility that infants may be interested in looking at displays that contain the parts of bodies (e.g., arms, legs, torso, head), without having a preference for how those parts are assembled, and (b) to allow for comparison with the body of literature on infants' responses to typical and scrambled faces.

Infants at 12, 15, and 18 months of age were presented with pairs of human body line drawings, one typical and one scrambled body per trial, for a total of six trials. Typical and scrambled schematic face stimuli were also presented, paired on a single looking trial. The results of this study revealed that 18-month-olds had a reliable looking preference for the scrambled body shapes over typical body shapes, but no preference for either type of face pattern. The younger infants, in contrast, did not show differential responding to the body stimuli, but showed reliable preferences

17

at 12 and 15 months for the typical face over the scrambled face. This clear dissociation in infants' responses to human face and body stimuli indicated that infants' learning about human faces and human bodies follow different developmental trajectories.

The results also supported the idea that detailed visuo-spatial knowledge of the human body develops relatively late in infancy; however, further research is necessary because the lack of a visual preference in younger infants is ambiguous. One interpretation is that the 12- and 15-month-olds showed no preference for typical or scrambled body shapes because they did not visually discriminate the two types of body shapes. An alternative interpretation, however, is that younger infants are capable of distinguishing between typical and scrambled body shapes, but they did not have an inherent preference for one type of body shape over the other. Thus the failure to exhibit a preference for typical or scrambled bodies in infants younger than 18 months is inconclusive, and further studies are required to establish when and how detailed visuo-spatial body knowledge emerges in development. We report a series of studies that addresses this question in the following two chapters.

Body Part Localization by Toddlers

In the neuropsychological literature discussed above, researchers make a distinction between body part localization tasks, in which participants are requested to point out a named body part, and body part naming tasks, in which participants are requested to provide a lexical label for a body part. Both tasks require some lexical–semantic knowledge, but the body part localization tasks are thought to specifically assess visuo-spatial body knowledge because in order to find a named body part, participants must have an intact topographical representation of where specific body parts are located in relation to the whole body.

Developmentally, these two tasks are not so easily separated because toddlers learn body parts by pointing and naming. Successful body part localization therefore depends on some level of developed lexical–semantic body knowledge. In the few developmental studies on this topic, the two tasks are often conflated and referred to as "body part identification," but since this review of literature adheres to the three-level model of human body knowledge, we discuss the development of body part localization and body part naming skills separately. Note that the interdependence of these skills indicates that these tasks involve developmentally more advanced human body knowledge at a symbolic representational level, compared to the visual discrimination tasks discussed in the previous sections.

The capacity to accurately point to body parts develops rapidly between the ages of 12 months and 4 years. The developmental sequence is fairly regular across children, such that several standardized developmental tests include some body part localization items (e.g., Bayley, 1969). Witt et al. (1990) undertook a detailed developmental study of body part identification in 11–25-month-olds by asking toddlers to point out 20 different body parts on a doll. Results indicated that only a minority of 12-month-olds accurately localized any body parts and those parts found first were parts of the face: eyes, hair, nose, and mouth. The first nonfacial body parts to be accurately localized were arm, hand, finger, legs, foot, toes and tummy, by a minority of toddlers at 15 months of age. Localization ability steadily increased after that such that by 24 months of age, 90% of toddlers were able to point to 11 or more body parts. At that age, the best performance was still on facial parts, with over 95% of the 24-month-olds capable of accurately pointing to eyes, hair, nose, and mouth.

Twenty-four-month-olds' ability to point to body parts on a doll and on themselves was also compared, revealing no difference between the two skills (Witt et al., 1990). Identical performance in body part naming across real humans and representations of humans is also seen in adult autotopagnosics, who typically perform identically on localization tasks involving real bodies or representations of bodies (but see Felician et al., 2003, discussed below). This equivalence of performance across real bodies and representations of bodies suggests the presence of a single visuo-spatial representation for all human bodies, including one's own, another's, body pictures and models. We return to this issue in the following chapters, with specific reference to infants' responses to different types of human body representations.

Toddlers' and Young Children's Human Figure Drawings

When toddlers begin to generate external representations in the second and third year of life, a common topic in their drawings is the human body, often one of the first images to be produced. These initial representations of humans are highly predictable both in terms of structure and development (Cox, 1993; Harris, 1963). An enduring question in this literature is whether children's human figure drawings reflect their human body knowledge, that is, are the drawings made with reference to a visuo-spatial body representation?

Around age two and a half, children first begin to draw "tadpole" people. These human figure drawings typically depict a head at the top of the figure, often with two dot eyes and a line mouth, and two legs descending from the head. Tadpole drawings continue to around age four, with some elaboration; arms may be added, usually extending from the sides of the head, and features like ears or hair may be added to the head. The basic shape of the tadpole figure, however, remains simple: a head with

19

symmetrical extensions below (Cox, 1993). After age four or so, children's drawings of the human figure become more detailed and most notably a torso is included. In a "transitional" figure, the torso is drawn with legs attached, but the arms are still portrayed as extending from the sides of the head. Finally, "conventional" human figure drawings include a torso from which the head and all four limbs extend. It is interesting to note that young children's human figure drawings in the early stages are almost invariably presented standing upright and facing forward; it is not until after age seven or so that children begin to depict humans in sitting postures, in movement, or in profile (Cox, 1993; Cox & Lambon, 1996).

As noted above, there is an ongoing debate about whether children's human figure drawings accurately reflect their knowledge of the human body. If children draw tadpole figures based on an internal representation, that suggests that toddlers' visuo-spatial knowledge of the human body is minimal, including only a head and some limbs below. Note that this is in line with Quinn and Eimas' (1998) proposal about the structure of infants' earliest representation of humans. Brittain and Chien's (1983) data are relevant here; these authors compared performance on human body drawing and body part localization tasks by asking toddlers who routinely drew tadpole figures to point to body parts on a pre-drawn detailed human figure. Tadpole drawers were able to identify hands, bellies, knees, etc., on those drawings even though they did not depict them in their own drawings. This suggests that toddlers' visuo-spatial body knowledge as required for localization tasks is more detailed than their drawings admit. Similarly, when tadpole drawers were given body parts to assemble in a paper-doll construction task, they made a conventional figure (e.g., one with head, arms, torso, legs) if the body parts in the construction task were accurately shaped and detailed (Cox, 1993). Again, these results suggest that toddlers have more detailed mental representations of the human figure than they are capable of depicting in their drawings. However, in a selection task in which children were asked to draw a human and then choose the best human from a range of tadpole, transitional and conventional human figure drawings, tadpole drawers chose tadpole figures over conventional figures as being the best picture of a person (Cox, 1993). Furthermore, individual children sometimes produce complex drawings that include several levels of human figure drawings, from tadpoles to conventional figures (Cox, 1993).

Given these data, the proposal that toddlers draw tadpole figures because they possess only a minimal or incomplete body representation seems unlikely; however, tadpole drawers only produce more complex human figures when they are prompted to do so via specific task demands. One interpretation is that the basic visuo-spatial body representation of toddlers is highly schematic like their tadpole drawings, but they also have access to more detailed information about the human figure. An alternate proposal is that children draw tadpoles solely because of performance constraints on drawing. On this view tadpole drawers have detailed body representations, but they are unable to plan and execute the drawing that would accurately depict their knowledge (Freeman, 1987). Cox (1993) similarly suggests that tadpole drawers have complete internal models, but suggests that children do not know how to pictorially depict all they know about the human figure. She argues that children's graphic human body representations reflect the relative salience of particular body parts, with head and legs being most important in the tadpole drawing stage. The idea that young children's body knowledge is hierarchically organized is consistent with the body part localization data, in which parts of the head and limbs were learned earlier than parts of the torso. Further, this hierarchy of body part salience also comes through in the development of lexical–semantic body knowledge, discussed below.

In this section, we have reviewed evidence for the development of visuo-spatial body knowledge in infancy and toddlerhood. This level of human body knowledge, like the sensori-motor level, involves different developmental levels of representation. The first evidence for visuo-spatial body knowledge comes from infants' early categorization of humans and animals; it was suggested that infants' performance on such tasks implicates the presence of an initial, schematic representation of the human body in the first six months of life (Quinn & Eimas, 1998). In the second year of life, infants discriminate typical from scrambled human bodies, indicating the likely presence of a detailed visuo-spatial human body representation that specifies how body parts relate to each other in the whole. Soon after that, toddlers begin to perform body part localization, which implicates both visuo-spatial body knowledge and the beginnings of lexical–semantic knowledge about the body. At yet another level, toddlers may demonstrate this level of human body knowledge through the production of human body drawings, which involve symbolic processing of visuo-spatial body representations.

EMERGENCE OF LEXICAL–SEMANTIC HUMAN BODY REPRESENTATIONS

Toddlers' Identification of Body Parts

Verbal knowledge about the structure of the human body emerges in the second year of life. Developmentally, this presents fairly clear cut evidence that the toddler is operating at a level of symbolic representation. The ability to name body parts develops rapidly between the ages of one and two years (Gesell, 1940) and shows an emergence hierarchy. Names for head and facial features are typically the first parts to be learned, followed by names for arms and legs and fingers and toes. Note that this developmental progression is perfectly consonant with the development of body part localization, reviewed above, perhaps not surprisingly because, as noted, toddlers' learning about body parts involves simultaneous learning of body part locations and names. Names for joints (e.g., wrist, elbow, knee) are learned later, as are terms that encompass a number of parts (e.g., body) and terms that refer to parts of parts (e.g., eyelash; Andersen, 1978; Witt, et al., 1990). Body part recall studies also reflect hierarchically organized lexical–semantic body part knowledge, as children are most likely to name parts of the head and face, and the feet, when asked to free recall parts of the body (Crowe & Prescott, 2003; Johnson, Perlmutter, & Trabasso, 1979).

The Acquisition of Knowledge About Human Body Function

Coincident with learning the names of body parts, toddlers start learning about the functions of some body parts as well. Functions of highly salient and visible parts, such as the sensory organs of the face, and the hands and feet, which all have easily identifiable and unique functions, are learned earlier than functions of other parts (Gellert, 1962; Jaakkola & Slaughter, 2002). There is a large and growing literature on the development of knowledge about the human body as a biological entity; this literature indicates that functional knowledge of some internal body parts is acquired in the preschool and early school years, and becomes elaborated as children construct a naive biological framework and as they participate in formal learning about the biology of the human body (Jaakkola & Slaughter, 2002; Inagaki & Hatano, 2002; see chapters in Siegal & Peterson, 1999). As any medical practitioner will attest, the acquisition of lexical–semantic knowledge about the human body is a lifelong developmental process.

SUMMARY AND CONCLUSIONS

This review of evidence for development of levels of human body knowledge in infancy and early childhood indicates that sensori-motor knowledge of the human body may originate in congenital intermodal co-ordinations, and those may form the basis for later-developing sensori-motor representations of the body. Visuo-spatial body knowledge is also evidenced at different developmental levels of complexity, from simple perceptual discriminations of humans versus animals, to discrimination of typical versus scrambled human bodies, to body part localization and finally human figure drawings. Last to develop appears to be lexical–semantic body knowledge, not surprisingly as this level relies solely on symbolic (language-based) representations.

In the remainder of this *Monograph*, we explore in more detail the development of visuo-spatial body representations. In the next two chapters, we report a series of studies that further investigate some of the issues that have been raised in the foregoing review, namely: At what age does detailed visuo-spatial knowledge of the human body emerge? What is the developmental trajectory for this level of human body knowledge? How is this level of knowledge of the body related to the well-documented phenomenon of precocious face recognition in infancy?

At the same time, we also consider theoretical accounts of how the three levels of human body representation may be related in development. As reviewed above, the three levels of human body knowledge we have reviewed are dissociable, both in adults as evidenced by neuroimaging and studies of patients with brain damage, and in infants (e.g., young infants possess sensori-motor knowledge but obviously lack lexical–semantic knowledge; this is generally true not only with respect to human body knowledge but in other content domains as well; Piaget, 1962; Müller & Overton, 1998). The neuropsychological evidence indicates that human body knowledge is widely distributed but also may occupy adjacent brain regions in the parietal lobe, suggesting that different levels of human body knowledge may be functionally related. We consider this possibility with respect to the developmental data in the final chapter.

NOTE

1. We recognize that within the developmental literature, a more common perspective is that representation involves not just any type of stored knowledge, but mental "representation" of previously perceived elements of experience (Piaget, 1962; Perner, 1991; Suddendorf & Whiten, 2001).

II. VISUAL HABITUATION STUDIES: INFANTS' RESPONSES TO TYPICAL AND SCRAMBLED BODY PICTURES

This series of studies explores the early development of visuo-spatial human body knowledge in infancy. To achieve this, infants' responses to typical and scrambled human body shapes were tested. As reviewed above, previous work showed that in a preferential looking paradigm, only 18-month-olds appeared to discriminate scrambled from typical human body shapes. This pattern is inconclusive, however, because a lack of preference in younger infants is ambiguous with respect to whether they can discriminate the two types of body shapes. The studies reported below utilized habituation procedures in which infants were presented with typical body shapes until habituation was established, then on the test trials scrambled body shapes were presented, to test for discrimination of the two types of body shapes.

The habituation studies were designed to incorporate the six typical and six scrambled body shapes used in our previous work. This is because, as noted above, those body shapes were originally created such that they make basic-level cuts in the body part hierarchy, and they control for overall amount of contour as well as for symmetry. Given the results of the visual preference studies, it was hypothesized that 18-month-olds, who preferred scrambled body shapes in the visual preference paradigm, would also discriminate typical and scrambled human body shapes in the habituation paradigm. Younger infants' performance was not predicted based on previous findings; thus the performance of 12- and 15-month-olds, who showed no visual preference for typical or scrambled body shapes, was of particular interest.

Typically, habituation procedures have not been used with infants older than 12 months of age. The relatively mature age of the sample and the decision to incorporate the six typical and six scrambled body shapes from previous work, constrained the design of the habituation studies somewhat. In order to get relatively mature, easily bored one-year-olds though the procedure, a minimal habituation paradigm was used whereby infants were

24

habituated to one type of body shape, then shown all six exemplars from the other body shape category.[2]

For all of the studies in this chapter, the basic procedure was similar: Infants were first habituated to a series of typical human body shapes. Habituation was defined as a 50% decrement in looking time during the first three trials over three subsequent trials. Once the habituation criterion was reached, then infants were shown the scrambled body test stimuli. In Studies 2 and 4, the test stimuli consisted of a single scrambled stimulus. In Studies 1, 3, and 5, the test stimuli consisted of a series of scrambled body shapes. Infants' looking times were coded into blocks: the first three trials (which represented the baseline for the habituation criterion), the final three habituation trials (which represented the 50% decrement in looking from baseline), and where appropriate, the first three dishabituation trials and the final three dishabituation trials. The analyses were conducted as follows: (a) a comparison of looking over the first three habituation trials compared to the final three habituation trials, to confirm that habituation genuinely occurred in any given condition, (b) a comparison of looking over the final three habituation trials compared to the first three dishabituation trials (where there was more than one scrambled test stimulus), to test for discrimination of the different body types, (c) a comparison of looking on the final habituation trial compared to looking on the initial dishabituation trial, to evaluate infants' initial responses to the new body type, and (d) comparison of looking on the first three dishabituation trials and the final three dishabituation trials (where there was more than one scrambled test stimulus), to explore infants' responses to repeated exposures to the new body types. The statistical analyses for each study reported below follow generally along these lines.

We also included nonparametric analyses to confirm the patterns found in the looking-time data. The idea was to classify infants as noticing or not noticing the transition to a new body type. One way to achieve this would have been to designate infants as noticing if they looked longer at the test stimuli. That would mean any increase in looking would constitute noticing, however that criterion struck us as too liberal because some infants recover looking by only 25 ms, whereas others recover by several seconds. Which infants genuinely noticed the new body type? We decided that the best approach would be to evaluate infants' looking patterns on previous habituation trials to assess how variable their looking was in the first place. To account for individual variation in looking behavior across infants, we used infants' own variability in looking as a criterion for passing. We therefore calculated the standard deviation of infants' final three habituation trials, and used that number to represent their individual looking variability when the patterns were all from the same body-type category (e.g., all typical bodies). If on the first test trial, their recovery in looking exceeded that standard deviation and their total recovery of looking was in excess of one second, then they were classified as noticing the new pattern. That means that they recovered interest to the new body type by an amount that exceeded their own established baseline variability in looking on the previous three trials. We took this as an acceptable measure of increase in looking; it is arbitrary but it takes infants' own looking patterns into account. For example, data for one 18-month-old's final three looking trials were 3388, 1294, and 384 ms, respectively. The *SD* for these scores is 1540 ms. This 1540 ms represents the average variation in looking when the patterns are similar. For this infant to qualify as a noticer, his looking time on the initial test trial had to increase by more than 1540 ms over the final habituation trial. This infants' looking time on the first test trial was 3873 ms, an increase in looking compared to the final habituation trial, but more importantly also an increase on his average variation in looking over the previous three trials.

We also included walking experience as a subject variable, based on the idea that sensori-motor, visuo-spatial and lexical–semantic levels of body knowledge may interact. As noted above, some authors suggest that the visuo-spatial and lexical–semantic levels of body knowledge may derive from or depend upon earlier-developing sensori-motor representations (Buxbaum & Coslett, 2001; Lefford, Birch, & Green, 1974; Poeck & Orgass, 1975). While there is currently no direct evidence for such an interaction of body knowledge in development, research with adult participants confirms that body knowledge may interact across levels. For example, Reed and Farah (1995) found that when adults moved their own bodies, their performance on a body picture matching task improved. Reed and Farah offered two interpretations of their data: They suggested that this might implicate a supramodal representation that codes simultaneously for one's own moving body and the spatial layout of the bodies of others, or alternatively it may implicate an interaction of sensori-motor and visuo-spatial representations of the body. On either interpretation, moving one's own body improves recognition of the bodies of others; by including walking as a variable in the visual discrimination studies, we investigate whether a similar effect might be evident in development.

Finally, gender was also included as a subject variable in all studies, based on reports that girls tend to outperform boys on body part localization tasks (e.g., MacWhinney, Cermak, & Fisher, 1987). This suggests that girls may acquire visuo-spatial body knowledge earlier than boys do.

STUDY 1: CATEGORICAL DISCRIMINATION OF SCHEMATIC HUMAN BODY SHAPES

The purpose of this study was to establish at what age infants first discriminate scrambled from typical human body shapes. Infants were shown a series of line drawings of typical human bodies in various postures, until they were habituated. Next, they were presented with a series of scrambled human body shapes. Looking times to all human body pictures were measured. On the basis of previous research (Slaughter et al., 2002) it was predicted that 18-month-olds, and possibly also younger infants, would show a recovery of interest upon presentation of the scrambled human body shapes. Such a discrimination would implicate the presence of a visuo-spatial representation of the body, as it involves infants' noticing violations of the canonical spatial layout of the human body.

Method

Participants

These were 20 12-month-olds (mean (M) age, 12 months and 4 days; range, 11 months 17 days to 12 months 16 days; 13 boys, 7 girls), 20 15-month-olds (M age, 15 months and 2 days; range, 14 months 16 days to 15 months 30 days; 9 boys and 11 girls), and 20 18-month-olds (M age, 18 months and 13 days; range 18 months 2 days to 18 months 21 days; 10 boys, 10 girls). An additional 12-month-old and two 15-month-olds were tested but excluded from the final sample due to excessive fussiness or experimenter error. In this study and the studies reported in the remainder of this chapter, excessive fussiness was defined behaviorally as a refusal to face forward in the highchair, and/or refusal to fixate the pictures on three consecutive trials, and/or inconsolable crying. Fussiness resulted in immediate termination of testing and all data were discarded.

Infants' names were taken from birth announcements of a local newspaper, or from an existing subject pool. Parents were contacted via mail and telephone and anyone who volunteered to participate did so. The sample was mainly Caucasian, living in suburbs around the Brisbane metropolitan area.

Materials

The stimuli consisted of six pictures depicting typical human bodies, and six pictures depicting scrambled human bodies. Pictures were black line drawings on white paper (30 cm × 21.5 cm). Excluding body shape and posture all drawings were identical. The six typical body pictures (left to right, top row of Figure 1) represented the human body in a variety of postures, including: (a) left leg bent at knee, shin parallel to the ground and right arm extended at 70°, left arm hanging by side, (b) feet shoulder width and arms hanging by sides, (c) feet shoulder width and arms extended from shoulders at 90°, forearms raised, (d) feet shoulder width and arms extended from shoulders at 70°, (e) feet shoulder width and arms raised above the head and (f) feet spread wide and arms hanging by sides. The scrambled body pictures (left to right, bottom row of Figure 1) represented violations of the typical human body shape, and were constructed by moving the limbs to noncanonical locations on the body, including (a) legs attached at shoulders and arms attached at hips, (b) feet shoulder width and arms attached at ears and raised upwards, (c) feet shoulder width and arms hanging by sides but right arm and leg switched, (d) feet shoulder width and arms attached at ears and hanging down, (e) feet shoulder width and arms hanging by sides but attached at hips, (f) arms, legs and head disconnected from the torso and floating in canonical positions.

Pictures were presented to the infant using a viewing screen (90 cm × 120 cm) that contained a single picture on the left-hand side of the screen. A piece of cardboard was used to cover the picture between trials. A hole in the middle of the screen allowed video recording of the infant.

An iMac was used to run the timing program that calculated infants' looking over trials and signalled with a single quiet beeping sound when the habituation criterion was met.

Procedure

On arrival at the university, the infant and mother were escorted to a room where the infant could play to warm up. Following this, they were brought to the testing room where the infant was seated in a high chair facing the viewing screen that was situated 1.5 m in front of the infant. The mother sat on the right of the infant facing away from the viewing screen. If the infant began to cry, or refused to stay seated in the infant seat, he/she was transferred to the mother's lap with both mother and infant facing the screen. In both instances mothers were requested not to speak or interact with their infants while the experiment was in progress. The experimenter was behind the apparatus (not visible to the infant). Individual trials began with the experimenter shaking a rattle to direct the infant's attention to the viewing screen, then lifting the covering cardboard to reveal the first human body picture. As soon as the picture was visible to the infant, the 15-second trial began. Once 15 s were passed the experimenter replaced the covering cardboard, changed pictures, then removed the cardboard again to begin the next trial. An infant controlled habituation method was employed (see Coding section for details). Infants viewed a minimum of six typical bodies, and a maximum of 12 typical bodies. Once habituation to typical bodies had occurred, the six scrambled body pictures were presented individually. The order of the typical body pictures presented was the same for each infant (if more than six were required to reach habituation the order of presentation of typical bodies was repeated). The order of scrambled bodies presented was rotated through a Latin Square across infants, so that the first scrambled picture shown to the infant moved to the last position and the second picture moved to the first position for the next infant and so on. The entire session lasted approximately 5–10 min.

Coding

Looking time was defined as the amount of time infants spent looking at the picture presented. Looking times were coded on line during the experiment using a computer program that calculated and averaged on-going looking times. Habituation was defined as a 50% decrement in looking time during the first three trials over three subsequent trials. Thus the minimum number of typical body looking trials was six (the three first trials, then three more trials to reach the 50% looking time criterion). Infants' looking times were recoded after the experiment was complete.

Twenty-five percent of the data were randomly recoded for reliability by a second coder who was naïve to the hypotheses under investigation. The agreement between the two coders was 88%. For statistical analysis, values were taken from the looking times recorded by the first observer. All looking times reported are in milliseconds.

Results and Discussion

Four 12-month-olds, one 15-month-old and two 18-month-olds did not provide data for the final 3 scrambled body trials. Their data on other trials were retained for analysis.

To confirm that the habituation criterion was met for the typical bodies, the mean looking times for the first three trials where typical bodies were presented were compared with mean looking times for the final three typical body trials. The respective means were as follows: 4390.73 ms ($SD = 2121.97$ ms) and 2296.20 ms ($SD = 1396.73$ ms) for the 12-month-olds, 7592.28 ms ($SD = 2675.05$ ms) and 3837.97 ms ($SD = 2276.94$ ms) for the 15-month-olds, and 8628.90 ms ($SD = 3297.68$ ms) and 3790.13 ms ($SD = 2472.45$ ms) for the 18-month-olds. These data indicate that infants showed a decrement in looking to the typical body pictures prior to presentation of the scrambled body pictures. The mean number of typical body trials required for the habituation criterion to be met was 8.35 ($SD = 2.31$), 7.90 ($SD = 2.42$) and 7.40 ($SD = 1.80$) for the 12-, 15- and 18-month-olds, respectively.

Next, infants' looking over the final three typical body trials was compared with their looking over the first three scrambled body trials, to test whether they noticed the transition from typical to scrambled body shapes. Looking times on the final three typical body trials and the initial three scrambled body trials were averaged and then treated as a repeated measure. To test whether infants dishabituated upon presentation of the scrambled body shapes, a 2 (gender) × 3 (age group: 12-, 15- and 18-month-olds) × 2 (body type: typical bodies vs. scrambled bodies) mixed model ANOVA was computed, where body type was a repeated measure and looking time was the dependent variable. This analysis revealed significant main effects for age, $F(2,54) = 23.30$, $p < .001$, $\eta^2 = .46$ and body type, $F(1,54) = 34.39$, $p < .001$, $\eta^2 = .39$, qualified by a significant age × body type interaction, $F(2,54) = 15.27$, $p < .001$, $\eta^2 = .36$. The interaction indicated that infants of different ages showed distinct patterns of responding to the introduction of scrambled bodies following the typical body presentations. Follow-up t-tests revealed significantly longer looking times for the scrambled bodies compared to the typical bodies for the 15-month-old infants, $t(19) = 2.73$, $p < .025$, (M, typical bodies 3837.96 ms, scrambled bodies 5360.36 ms; $SD = 1805.77$ ms, 2565.67 ms, respectively) and the 18-month-old infants, $t(19) = 6.25$, $p < .001$, (M, typical bodies 3790.13 ms, scrambled bodies 7503.12 ms; $SD = 1456.10$ and 3257.25 ms, respectively). The 12-month-olds showed no significant difference in looking to the typical and scrambled bodies $t(19) = .81$, ns, (M, typical bodies 2296.20 ms, scrambled bodies 2092.68 ms; $SD = 822.76$ and 798.50 ms, respectively). This pattern indicated that infants of 15 and 18 months of age were sensitive to the transition from typical human bodies to scrambled human bodies. The 12-month-olds, in contrast, did not notice that transition.

Next a similar analysis was performed comparing infants' looking on the final typical body presentation and the first scrambled body presentation. This comparison is less conservative than the previous one, because it compares looking on the final, most "boring" typical body trial, with looking on the initial scrambled body trial, where a novel stimulus has first been introduced. A 2 (gender) × 3 (age group: 12-, 15- and 18-month-olds) × 2 (body type: typical vs. scrambled body) mixed model ANOVA was computed, where body type was a repeated measure and looking time was the dependent variable. Results revealed significant main effects for age, $F(2,54) = 15.60$, $p < .001$, $\eta^2 = .37$, and for the repeated measure body type, $F(1,54) = 37.83$, $p < .001$, $\eta^2 = .41$, qualified by a significant age × body type interaction, $F(2,54) = 8.98$, $p < .001$, $\eta^2 = .25$. Again, the significant age by body type interaction indicated that infants' change in looking times from the typical to scrambled body pictures varied by age group. Follow-up t-tests indicated significantly longer looking times for the first scrambled body compared to the final typical body for the 15-month-old infants,

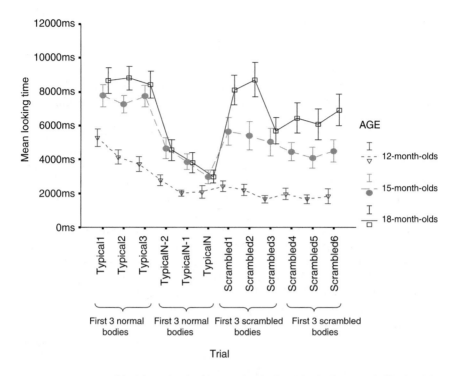

FIGURE 2.—Looking times for the first 3 typical body trials, the last 3 typical body trials and the 6 scrambled body trials by age group in Study 1.

$t(19) = 2.98$, $p < .005$ (M, typical body 2976.55 ms, scrambled body 5655.20 ms; $SD = 1744.85$ and 3626.38 ms respectively) and the 18-month-old infants, $t(19) = 5.58$, $p < .001$, (M, typical body 2999.75 ms, scrambled body 8101.70 ms; $SD = 1727.86$ and 3879.83 ms, respectively). Thus the older infants were immediately sensitive to the transition from typical to scrambled human body shapes. The 12-month-olds showed no significant difference in looking upon presentation of the first scrambled body, $t(19) = 1.08$, ns, (M, typical body 2082.25 ms, scrambled body 2422.80 ms; $SD = 1738.37$ and 1461.52 ms, respectively). Figure 2 shows the looking times for the first three typical body trials, the last three typical body trials and the six scrambled body trials, by age group. This figure makes it graphically clear that the 12-month olds, in contrast to the older infants, did not dishabituate, even upon presentation of the initial scrambled human body.

An examination of individual infants' looking patterns to the typical and scrambled body line drawings revealed that of the 12-month-old infants,

31

three of the 20 infants (15%) looked longer (by our criterion described above) at the first scrambled body picture than the final typical body picture. In contrast, 10 of the 20 15-month-old infants (50%) looked longer at the first scrambled body picture compared to the final typical body picture, and 18 of the 20 18-month-old infants (90%) noticed the first scrambled body picture by our criterion. This pattern confirms that seen in the looking-time data, and indicates that sensitivity to scrambled human body shapes is not evident at 12 months of age, but increases between the ages of 15 and 18 months.

As noted above, there is reason to hypothesize that sensori-motor and visuo-spatial body knowledge may interact, so in accordance with this idea, the results for the 12-month-olds were further analyzed with respect to whether or not the infants had begun walking. A 2 (walking or not) × 2 (body type: final typical versus first scrambled) mixed model ANOVA with body type as the repeated measure was run on the 12-month-old's looking time data. The purpose of this analysis was to explore whether upright motor experience would be related to infants' capacity to discriminate scrambled from typical bodies. The ANOVA revealed a significant walking by body shape interaction, $F(1,18) = 7.82$, $p < .02$, $\eta^2 = .08$, suggesting that infants' walking status was related to their dishabituation responses. Follow-up paired t-tests indicated that infants who were walking showed a significant increase in looking to the scrambled body shape, paired $t(9) = 2.56$, $p < .05$, (M, typical body 1729.70 ms, scrambled body 2826.90 ms; $SD = 845.32$ and 1297.43 ms respectively), while infants who were not yet walking did not significantly dishabituate to the scrambled body, paired $t(9) = 1.26$, ns, (M, typical body 2434.80 ms, scrambled body 2018.70 ms; $SD = 1569.50$ and 2321.39 ms, respectively). Further, all three 12-month-olds who noticed the transition to scrambled body shapes according to the nonparametric analysis presented above, were already walking. These data indicate that that those 12-month-olds who were walking were more likely to be sensitive to the transition from typical to scrambled human body shapes than their nonwalking peers, suggesting that walking experience may be related to the early development of a visuo-spatial human body representation. However, it should be noted that those infants who were relatively early walkers may also have been relatively accelerated in a number of developmental domains besides gross motor development. Thus while this analysis tentatively suggests a link between sensori-motor body representations, implicated in motor development, and visuo-spatial body representations, implicated in the visual discrimination of scrambled from typical body shapes, the issue requires further study.

In the next analysis, infants' dishabituation was investigated with respect to the specific scrambled body shape presented in the first scrambled body trial. This analysis was performed in order to explore whether any

TABLE 1

MEAN DIFFERENCE SCORES (IN MILLISECONDS) COMPARING LOOKING TIMES TO
FINAL TYPICAL BODIES VERSUS THE FIRST SCRAMBLED BODIES, BY SCRAMBLED BODY SHAPE
IN STUDY 1

Scrambled Shape	Mean Difference (ms)	df	t-Value
Averaged total	− 2707.05	59	− 5.40**
Arms raised from head	− 3959.00	8	− 2.44*
Arms hanging from hips	− 3513.50	7	− 2.34*
Limbs disconnected	− 1871.89	8	− 1.63
Both arms/legs switched	− 3924.83	11	− 3.30**
One arm/one leg switched	− 277.22	8	− .33
Arms hanging from head	− 2480.31	12	− 2.60*

*$p < .05$.
**$p < .01$.

particular scrambled body shape was more or less salient than the others. Infants of all ages were included in this analysis to increase power. Table 1 shows that infants dishabituated significantly to all of the scrambled body shapes except the one leg/arm switch figure (third from left, bottom row Figure 1) and the limbs disconnected figure (far right, bottom row Figure 1). These two scrambled bodies, therefore, appear to be less salient than the other four scrambled bodies; this is not surprising as these two scrambled bodies are arguably less monstrous than the rest; the one leg/arm switch figure requires detailed inspection to notice the limb switch, and the limbs disconnected figure does not violate the canonical locations for the head and limbs, it simply disconnects them from the torso. Thus this analysis provides some evidence for a continuum of saliency for human body violations; all scrambled bodies are not created equal.

Finally, infants' responses to the six scrambled bodies in the dishabituation phase were investigated. A 2 (gender) × 3 (age group: 12-, 15- and 18-month-olds) × 2 (presentation: first three scrambled bodies vs. final 3 scrambled bodies) ANOVA was computed with presentation as the repeated measure and looking time as the dependent variable. This analysis revealed a significant main effect of age, $F(2,47) = 30.55$, $p < .001$, $\eta^2 = .57$, and a marginal effect of presentation, $F(1,47) = 3.60$, $p < .07$, $\eta^2 = .07$. Follow-up t-tests investigating the effect of presentation revealed that infants at all ages looked longer at the first three scrambled bodies compared to the final three scrambled bodies, $t(52) = 2.02$, $p < .05$ (M, first three scrambled bodies 9082.16 ms, last three scrambled bodies 4370.16 ms, $SDs = 3239.89$ ms and 2687.06 ms, respectively). This pattern reflects a new habituation process (to the category of scrambled bodies) for the older infants, and continuing decrement in looking for the 12-month-olds.

Overall, the results of Study 1 confirm that, as predicted from the visual preference work, 18-month-olds discriminate between typical and scrambled human body shapes. The results further indicate that 15-month-olds are sensitive to violations of the typical human body shape, evidenced by their recovery of interest following the transition from typical to scrambled body shapes. Infants of 12 months, on the other hand, did not, as a group, show recovery of interest when scrambled body shapes were presented, although the subset of 12-month-olds who were walking did show evidence of discrimination of scrambled from typical body shapes. This walking effect is reminiscent of Reed and Farah's (1995) finding of a facilitating interaction between body movement and body perception in adults, but as noted above, the developmental data must be interpreted with caution.

Thus it appears that both 15- and 18-month-olds have a visuo-spatial representation of the human body that supports a categorical discrimination between typical body shapes and scrambled body shapes. We argue that this is a categorical discrimination because in order to notice a difference between the first set of (typical) bodies and the second (scrambled) set, infants had to generalize across exemplars (e.g., the six individual typical bodies in different poses) and then recognize the scrambled bodies as non-members of the typical human body category. This means that the visuo-spatial knowledge of infants 15 months of age and older, is flexible enough to allow generalized recognition of the typical human body shape across different postures. Infants may acquire this human body knowledge on-line during the experimental procedure, or alternatively they may have come to the experiment with an already established visuo-spatial representation of the human body. This study does not allow us to distinguish between these two developmental alternatives; we return to this issue in Study 5 below.

The 12-month-olds' failure to discriminate between scrambled and typical human body shapes suggests two interpretations. The first is that at 12 months of age infants (as a group—we are putting aside the walking effect for the moment) have some visuo-spatial knowledge of the body, but it is not detailed enough to do the scrambled versus typical body discrimination task. Alternatively, it is possible that 12-month-olds have not yet acquired any human body knowledge at the visuo-spatial level. We discuss these two alternatives in more detail below.

STUDY 2: 12-MONTH-OLDS' DISCRIMINATION OF INDIVIDUAL SCHEMATIC HUMAN BODY SHAPES

The results of Study 1 suggested that infants develop a detailed visuo-spatial representation of the typical human body by age 15 months. This conclusion was based on the fact that infants of that age made a categorical discrimination between typical and scrambled bodies in the visual habituation task. However, in order to confirm that the 15- and 18-month-olds make a such a discrimination, that the 12-month-olds fail to make, it is necessary to run a control study showing that young infants are capable of discriminating between individual exemplars within the two categories.[3] If the youngest infants discriminate between two different typical bodies or two different scrambled bodies, but not between typical and scrambled bodies by group, that would demonstrate that they are capable of perceptually discriminating human body shapes, but lack a visuo-spatial human body representation that engenders categorization of those shapes as being typical or scrambled. It would also support the claim that older infants' discrimination of scrambled versus typical body shapes is indeed categorical, as older infants should be able to make a simple perceptual discrimination between individual bodies as well as their younger counterparts. Thus Study 2 addressed the following question: Can 12-month-old infants make a simple perceptual discrimination between two individual human body shapes, even though they do not make a categorical discrimination between typical and scrambled body shapes in general?

Method

Participants

Infants were recruited in a manner identical to that of Study 1. For the typical body discrimination task, there were 12 infants ranging in age from 11 months 20 days to 12 months 20 days, M age 12 months 5 days. There were five boys and seven girls. For the scrambled body discrimination task there were 12 infants ranging in age from 11 months 14 days to 12 months 14 days, M age 12 months 2 days. There were four boys and eight girls.

Materials

Stimuli were the human body line drawings used in Study 1 (see Figure 1).

Procedure

Study 2 used a standard habituation/dishabituation procedure. In the typical body discrimination task, infants were presented with a single typical human body shape (from the top row of Figure 1) repeatedly until the

35

habituation criterion was met. Trials were seven seconds each in length (shorter than the previous experiment because the task was more boring). Habituation was defined as a 50% decrement of looking from the first two trials (averaged) to a subsequent two trials. Thus four was the minimum habituation trials, and infants were shown a maximum of 10 trials; even if the habituation criterion was not met after 10 trials, the test stimuli were presented.

On the first test trial, a novel typical body shape (also from the top row of Figure 1) was presented. Following this, the familiar typical body picture was again presented. These trials were also seven seconds long.

The scrambled body discrimination task was identical with the exception that the two pictures presented to infants were scrambled bodies from the bottom row of Figure 1. Thus, one scrambled body picture was presented repeatedly during the habituation phase and a novel scrambled body picture was presented for the test trial. Following this, the familiar scrambled picture was again presented.

Given that in each condition (typical and scrambled) there were six different body pictures, it was not possible to exhaustively pair the pictures within categories. Therefore each infant saw two pictures (one as the habituation stimulus and one as the test stimulus) and counterbalancing ensured that each picture served once as the habituation stimulus and once as the test stimulus, across infants. Aside from this constraint, the pairing of pictures was random.

Coding

Infants' looking across all trials was timed and a naive viewer recoded all trials (because the looking times were quite short in this study, we performed reliability on 100% of the data to ensure that the results were accurate). Inter-coder reliability was 87% and as before, values were taken from the looking times recorded by the first observer. All looking times reported are in milliseconds.

Results and Discussion

Three infants were omitted due to fussiness (two from the typical discrimination task and one from the scrambled discrimination task).

The mean number of trials to habituation across both tasks was 5.13 ($SD = 1.15$). To ensure that infants were genuinely habituated, the means for the first two typical body trials and the final two typical body trials were compared. We compared the first and last two trials, rather than three as in Study 1, because habituation occurred more quickly in this procedure. For the first two trials of the typical discrimination task, the mean looking time was 3387.3 ms (SD = 1063.9 ms) and for the final two trials the mean looking time was 1228.7 ms (SD = 813.6 ms). For the first two trials for the scrambled discrimination task, the mean looking time was 2313.5 ms (SD = 1045.5 ms) and for the final two trials the mean looking time was 1150.1 ms (SD = 885.9 ms). These numbers confirm that infants met the habituation criterion of 50% decrement in looking before they were presented with the test trials.

Pre-planned paired t-tests were conducted to evaluate infants' responses to the novel picture presented in the test trial compared with their responses to the last picture presented during habituation. For the typical body discrimination task, this analysis revealed that infants looked significantly longer at the novel typical body compared to the familiar typical body, $t(11) = 3.03$, $p < .02$, ($M =$ familiar typical body 1113.42 ms, novel typical body 2954.00 ms; $SD = 1198.06$ ms, 1692.51 ms, respectively). This indicated that infants noticed the difference between the two individual typical body pictures. A comparison between the novel typical body and the subsequent familiar typical body (presented directly after the novel typical body) revealed that infants showed a significant decrement in looking to the repeated presentation of the familiar typical body compared with their previous looking time to the novel typical body, $t(11) = -4.03$, $p < .01$, (M novel typical body 2954.00 ms, familiar typical body 912.42 ms; $SD = 1692.51$ and 1195.67 ms, respectively). This indicated that infants' recovery of interest to the novel typical body on the previous trial was a genuine recovery of interest to a new pattern, rather than a response to the novelty of the picture changing procedure.

The scrambled body discrimination task revealed the same pattern of responding: Infants looked significantly longer at the novel scrambled body compared to the final presentation of the familiar scrambled body, $t(11) = 3.03$, $p < .02$ (M, familiar scrambled body 1197.00 ms, novel scrambled body 2448.42 ms; $SD = 618.77$ and 1257.65 ms, respectively). They also showed a decrement in looking to the re-presentation of the familiar scrambled body, compared with their previous looking at the novel scrambled body, $t(11) = -2.14$, $p < .057$, (M, novel scrambled body 2448.42 ms, familiar scrambled body 1452.92 ms; $SD = 1257.65$ and 1522.61 ms, respectively).

This pattern of responding was confirmed with our nonparametric analysis. An examination of individual infants' looking patterns to the last familiar individual body picture and the novel individual body picture revealed that for the typical body discrimination task, 10 of the 12 infants (83%) looked longer at the novel body compared to the last familiar body. For the scrambled body task, eight of the 12 infants (67%) looked longer at the novel scrambled body compared to the last familiar scrambled body.

37

Thus the pattern of data from Study 2 demonstrated that 12-month-old infants can discriminate between two individual human body pictures. Comparing the result of Studies 1 and 2, it appears that at 12 months, infants can detect a change in the configuration of the human body shape; they notice when an individual typical body changes postures (in the typical body discrimination task) or when an individual scrambled body looks different (in the scrambled body discrimination task). However, 12-month-old infants do not have access to a categorical representation of the typical human body shape that could support discrimination of scrambled from typical human body shapes, as required in Study 1.

We did not include older infants in this study because Study 1 showed that by 15 months, infants are capable of making the more complex discrimination between scrambled and typical human body shapes. Additionally, pilot testing indicated that this simple task was so boring that 15-month-olds would not sit through it. We, therefore, assume that if 12-month-olds can make the simple perceptual discrimination between two individual body shapes, then so should 15- and 18-month-olds. This assumption supports our claim that the older infants in Study 1 were responding categorically to the typical and scrambled body shapes presented. Again, these data suggest that by 15 months, infants possess a visuo-spatial representation of the typical spatial layout of the human body that allows them to discriminate scrambled from typical human bodies.

STUDY 3: CATEGORICAL DISCRIMINATION OF HUMAN BODY PHOTOGRAPHS

The pattern of data in the previous two studies suggests that 12-month-olds, perhaps surprisingly, do not categorically discriminate scrambled from typical human body shapes. Our interpretation of these data is that before 15 months of age, infants lack a detailed representation of the spatial layout of the human body. There is an alternative interpretation, however. It is possible that in the previous studies, 12-month-old infants did not recognize the schematic line drawings as portraying human bodies. This interpretation implies that whatever knowledge infants have about the human body, it did not come to bear on their performance in Studies 1 and 2, instead they were simply responding to meaningless black and white patterns on paper.

Our purpose is to understand how knowledge about the human body originates and develops, with a particular focus on the visuo-spatial level of body knowledge. This knowledge should be relevant to all sorts of human bodies, from the schematic stimuli we have thus far presented, to real human bodies, although ultimately the question of whether and when human body knowledge generalizes across stimulus types is an open empirical one. As reviewed in Chapter 1, there is good reason to believe that in older children and adults, human body knowledge does generalize across all sorts of stimulus types: 2-year-olds localize body parts equally well on their own bodies and dolls' bodies (Witt et al., 1990), and autotopagnosic adults similarly show equivalent responding across different types of human body stimuli (Denes et al., 2000; Guariglia, et al., 2002; Ogden, 1985). However, the two studies presented in this monograph thus far involve infants and toddlers younger than age two, and this may be important because the third year of life marks important changes in the development of children's capacity to understand and make use of external representations (DeLoache, 1995; Perner, 1991; Suddendorf, 2003). While the human body line drawings used in Studies 1 and 2 are easily recognized by adults as depictions of human bodies, it is possible that the same is not true of young infants. Casual observation from our lab suggests that at least some of the infants in Studies 1 and 2 immediately recognized the line drawings as human male figures; a number of infants responded to the line drawings with excited pointing that suggested recognition of the typical human as such, and more than one infant responded to the first typical body by declaring "Daddy."

Despite these observations, it remains a possibility that infants would respond differently if the stimuli were real humans. It is conceivable that the poor performance of 12-month-olds on the discrimination task derives somehow from a failure to recognize the line drawings in Figure 1 as representations of human bodies. It is also conceivable that the good performance of older infants could be affected if the task involved more realistic human body stimuli. Since it is not possible to scramble real human bodies, we addressed this issue by replicating Study 1, with an important difference, namely, the human body stimuli in Study 3 were color photographic images (instead of black and white line drawings), projected on large viewing screens to create relatively realistic, closer to life-sized, human body images. This procedure was also carried out in Slaughter et al.'s (2002) studies; there we found no difference in responding when the stimuli were human body line drawings versus photographs, but that study was limited in that it involved only a small sample of 12- and 18-month-olds, who were tested in a visual preference procedure. Thus Study 3 addressed the question of whether 12-, 15- and 18-month-olds' discrimination of scrambled from typical body shapes would be influenced by the realism of the human body stimuli.

Method

Participants

Infants were recruited in a manner identical to that of Study 1. Statistical analyses were based on a total of 59 infants. These included 20 12-month-olds (*M* age, 12 months and 7 days; range, 11 months 17 days to 12 months 20 days; 11 boys, 9 girls), 20 15-month-olds (*M* age, 15 months and 4 days; range, 14 months 14 days to 15 months 19 days; 10 boys, 10 girls) and 19 18-month-olds (*M* age, 18 months, 10 days, range 18 months 0 days to 18 months 21 days; 10 boys and nine girls). An additional five 12-month-olds and seven 15-month-olds were tested but excluded from the final sample due to excessive fussiness.

Materials

The stimuli were identical to those of Study 1 with respect to body shape (both typical and scrambled). However, these human body images were enlarged color photographs projected onto a screen instead of line drawings. Typical body photographs depicted a young adult human male of average stature and weight wearing black boy-leg swimming togs. Scrambled photos were created by scrambling the photograph of the typical human body using Adobe Photoshop software. See Figure 3 for the typical and scrambled human body photographs.

Procedure

The procedure was identical to Study 1 with the following exceptions. Images of body shapes were projected onto a large screen (100 cm ×

FIGURE 3.—Typical and scrambled body photographs used in Studies 3 and 4.

40

130 cm) thus pictures were substantially larger in size (42 cm × 55 cm) than in Study 1. Room lighting was dimmed to provide clearer images on the screen. Infants' attention was directed to the pictures by the clicking sound of the pictures being changed by the projector, thus the rattle was not necessary. The infant laboratory layout was identical to that of Study 1, with the exception that the video camera was positioned to the right of the screen and the infant. The entire session lasted approximately 5–10 min.

Coding

Coding of data was identical to that of Study 1. Inter-coder reliability on 25% of the data was calculated at 89%. All looking times reported are in milliseconds.

Results and Discussion

Six infants did not finish all trials; three 12-month-olds and three 15-month-olds provided no data for the final three scrambled body trials. Their data were retained for partial analysis.

To check that infants were successfully habituated to the typical body images, the average looking times for the first three typical body trials were compared to the average looking times for the final three typical body trials. The respective means were as follows: 4519.78 ms $(SD = 1979.71$ ms) and 2448.37 ms $(SD = 1717.11$ ms) for the 12-month-olds, 4391.17 ms $(SD = 1780.34$ ms) and 2171.83 ms $(SD = 1005.06$ ms) for the 15-month-olds, and 7690.38 ms $(SD = 1843.83$ ms) and 3275.42 ms $(SD = 1420.01$ ms) for the 18-month-olds. These numbers indicate that all infants habituated successfully to the typical body pictures. The average number of typical body trials to habituation was 8.39 $(SD = 2.47)$ across all three age groups.

To test whether infants dishabituated upon presentation of the scrambled body shapes, a 2 (gender) × 3 (age group: 12-, 15- and 18-month-olds) × 2 (body type: typical bodies versus scrambled bodies) mixed model ANOVA was computed, where body type was the repeated measure. The dependent variable was looking times averaged over the last three typical body trials and the first three scrambled body trials. This analysis revealed a pattern similar to that seen in Study 1: there were significant main effects for age, $F(2,53) = 14.56$, $p < .001$, $\eta^2 = .36$ and body type, $F(1,53) = 13.59$, $p < .001$, $\eta^2 = .20$, as well as a significant age × body type interaction, $F(2, 53) = 12.49$, $p < .001$, $\eta^2 = .32$. This interaction indicated that infants of different ages showed distinct patterns of responding to the scrambled bodies following the typical body presentations. Follow-up t-tests comparing the average looking times over the final three typical body trials versus looking over the initial three scrambled body trials indicated that the 18-month-olds looked significantly longer at the scrambled bodies compared to the typical bodies, $t(18) = 4.54$, $p < .001$, (M, typical bodies 3275.42 ms, scrambled bodies 5621.88 ms, $SD = 1420.01$ and 2279.32 ms, respectively). This finding replicates the performance of 18-month-olds in Study 1. Neither the 15-month-olds nor the 12-month-olds looked significantly longer at the scrambled bodies compared to the typical bodies in this study: both $t(19) = 1.55$, ns, (15-month-olds M, typical bodies 2171.83 ms, scrambled bodies 2650.07 ms; $SD = 1005.06$ and 1618.55 ms, respectively and 12-month-olds M, typical bodies 2448.37 ms, scrambled bodies 2089.27 ms, $SD = 1717.11$ and 1468.56 ms, respectively). This pattern differs from that found in Study 1; here the 15-month-olds failed to make the scrambled body-typical body discrimination, though they were successful in Study 1 when the stimuli were schematic line drawings. The performance of 12-month-olds did not change as a function of presenting realistic human body photographs; they failed to discriminate scrambled from typical bodies in both studies, even though a comparison of average looking times on the first three typical body trials in Study 1 compared to those in the current study indicated that 12-month-olds looked nearly twice as long at the photographs compared to the line drawings, $t(38) = 5.05$, $p < .01$. Thus although the 12-month-olds were apparently interested in the photographic images, this did not affect their performance on the discrimination task. This pattern of similar performance in responses to human body line drawings and photographs was also found in Slaughter et al. (2002).

Next the less conservative discrimination analysis was performed by comparing infants' looking at the final typical body picture versus the first scrambled body picture. A 2 (gender) × 3 (age group: 12-, 15- and 18-month-olds) × 2 (body type: final typical vs. first scrambled) mixed model ANOVA was computed, where body type was a repeated measure and looking time was the dependent variable. Results again revealed significant main effects for age, $F(2,53) = 14.13$, $p < .001$, $\eta^2 = .35$, and body type, $F(1,53) = 16.36$, $p < .001$, $\eta^2 = .24$, qualified by a significant interaction of age and body type, $F(2,53) = 9.21$, $p < .001$, $\eta^2 = .11$. There was also a three-way age by gender by body type interaction, $F(2,53) = 3.30$, $p < .05$, but given that gender was nonsignificant in all other studies and analyses, this effect was not interpreted. The significant age by body type interaction indicated that infants' looking to the initial scrambled body pictures varied by age group. Follow-up paired t-tests comparing infants' looking at the final typical body picture versus the first scrambled body picture confirmed the pattern from the previous analysis: only the 18-month-olds significantly increased their looking from the final typical body to the initial scrambled body, $t(18) = 3.36$, $p < .025$ (M, typical body 2820.11 ms, scrambled body

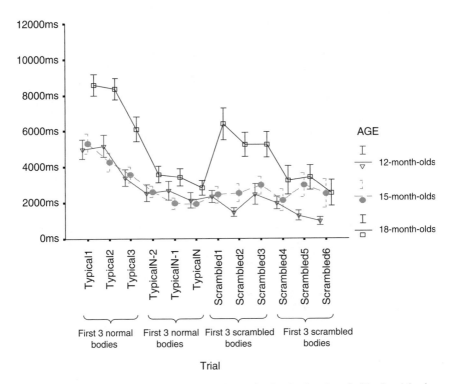

FIGURE 4.—Mean looking times (in milliseconds) for the first 3 typical body trials, the last 3 typical body trials and the 6 scrambled body trials for each age group in Study 3.

6394.53 ms; $SD = 1777.62$ and 3859.04 ms, respectively). The 15- and 12-month-olds again showed no significant increase in looking upon presentation of the first scrambled body, both $t(19) = 1.20$, ns (15-month-olds' M, typical bodies 1946.15 ms, scrambled bodies 2443.25 ms; $SD = 1134.02$ and 2070.11 ms, respectively and 12-month-olds M, typical bodies 2132.45 ms, scrambled bodies 2348.40 ms, $SD = 1909.16$ and 1499.17 ms, respectively). Figure 4 portrays the looking times across the first three typical body trials, the last three typical body trials and the six scrambled body trials, by age group.

An examination of individual infants' looking patterns to the typical and scrambled body photographs revealed that of the 12-month-old infants, three of the 20 infants (15%) looked longer at the first scrambled body picture than the final typical body picture. For the 15-month-old infants, five of the 20 infants (25%) looked longer at the first scrambled body picture than the final typical body picture. For the 18-month-old infants, 10 of the 19 infants (53%) looked longer at the first scrambled body picture

43

than the final typical body picture. These data confirmed that younger infants did not notice the transition to scrambled bodies, and also indicated that older infants were less likely to meet the criterion for noticing the transition to scrambled bodies in this study, compared with Study 1. Overall, the data suggest that the use of photographic human body images made the discrimination task somewhat more difficult for the older infants.

Next, the results for the 12-month-olds were analyzed with respect to whether or not the infants had begun walking, to attempt to confirm the finding from Study 1 that 12-month-old walkers were more likely to discriminate scrambled from typical body shapes. A 2 (walking or not) × 2 (body shape: typical versus scrambled) mixed model ANOVA with body shape as the repeated measure was computed for the 12-month-olds' looking-time data. Contrary to the results of Study 1, no main effects or interactions were significant (walking × body shape interaction, $F(1,18) = .001$, ns, $\eta^2 = 0$. Given that the 15-month-olds in this study also failed to dishabituate to the scrambled bodies, a similar analysis was run whereby 15-month-olds were classified as early walkers (more than 12 weeks experience walking at the time of testing; $n = 10$) or late walkers (fewer than 12 weeks experience at the time of testing, $n = 10$). A 2 (early vs. late walker) × 2 (body shape: typical vs. scrambled) mixed model ANOVA with body shape as the repeated measure was computed for the 15-month-olds' looking-time data. Again, no main effects or interactions were significant; walking × body shape interaction, $F(1,18) = 1.28$, ns, $\eta^2 = .07$. These results indicated that in the current sample and task, there was no relation between upright motor experience and discrimination of scrambled from typical human body shapes.

Finally, infants' looking at the first three scrambled bodies versus the final three scrambled bodies was investigated with a 3 (age group) by 2 (gender) by 2 (presentation: first three scrambled vs. final three scrambled) repeated measures ANOVA. This analysis revealed main effects for age, $F(2,47) = 9.45$, $p < .01$, $\eta^2 = .28$ and body type, $F(2,47) = 19.14$, $p < .001$, $\eta^2 = .29$, as well as a significant interaction of age and body type, $F(2,47) = 6.62$, $p < .01$, $\eta^2 = .22$. Follow-up t-tests indicated that there was a significant decrease in looking time for the final three scrambled body trials compared to the first three scrambled body trials for the 12-month-olds, $t(16) = 2.54$, $p < .025$ (M, first three scrambled bodies 2089.27 ms, last three scrambled bodies 1451.45 ms, $SD = 1468.56$ and 881.99 ms, respectively) and for the 18-month-olds, $t(18) = 4.12$, $p < .001$, (M, first three scrambled bodies 5621.88 ms, last three scrambled bodies 3061.18 ms, $SD = 2279.32$ and 2691.58 ms, respectively). The 15-month-olds, in contrast, showed no decrement in looking over the six scrambled body trials, (M, first three scrambled bodies 2650.07 ms, last three scrambled bodies

2537.72 ms, $SD = 1618.55$ and 2422.42 ms, respectively). This pattern indicates that the 15-month-olds, as a group, retained interest in the scrambled body photographs across the six test trials; this is different from their responses to the schematic body line drawings in Study 1. This pattern is hard to interpret but could indicate that the 15-month-olds in this study were actively processing the scrambled body photographs in an attempt to make sense of the images.

Overall, this study fairly closely replicated the pattern of data found in Study 1; 12-month-olds showed no evidence of discrimination between scrambled and typical human body shapes, while 18-month-olds demonstrated a healthy recovery of interest when presented with scrambled human body shapes following habituation to typical human body shapes. In the current study, 15-month-olds did not significantly dishabituate to scrambled human body shapes and this is in contrast to the results of Study 1 in which 15-month-olds showed weak but significant recovery of interest when scrambled body line drawings were presented. This indicates that 15-month-olds' capacity to discriminate scrambled from typical human bodies is affected by the realism of the body stimuli. The nonparametric analyses suggest that the same is true of 18-month-olds; fewer of the oldest infants met the criterion for noticing the first scrambled body photograph than met the criterion for noticing the first scrambled body line drawing in Study 1. Several features of the Study 3 display may be relevant to this stimulus effect: The photographs were larger, colorful and more detailed. It may be that a single one of these features affected 15-month-olds' responding. Alternatively it may be that the combination of features, which all contributed to the realism of the photographs of Study 3 compared to the line drawings of Study 1, was effective. As noted, 12-month-olds looked longer at the first typical body image when it was a color photo (Study 3) compared to a line drawing (Study 1); suggesting that the color photos were indeed more complex, more interesting or both. However, despite this stimulus effect, 12-month-olds' performance on the discrimination task was unaffected. Further, 15-month-olds' looking times to the initial three typical body stimuli were not significantly different in Study 1 and Study 3, but their discrimination performance did change across studies. This complex pattern suggests that stimulus realism is an important variable to consider, even if it does not account for the 15-month-olds' change in performance from Study 1 to Study 3.

Felician et al. (2003) also found a stimulus realism effect for human body task performance in their case study of an autotopagnosic individual. The patient was unusual in that she was unable to localize body parts on another person, but at the same time could localize body parts on a human body picture or video image. Relevant to the issue at hand, this pattern suggested a possible dissociation in visuo-spatial knowledge of real human bodies and representations of human bodies. Felician et al. (2003) discounted the idea of separate visuo-spatial body knowledge stores for real bodies and representations of bodies, and instead suggested that this apparent dissociation stemmed from the fact that real bodies are more perceptually complex and therefore likely to require more attention for visual processing. They hypothesized that the task dissociation they found may reflect a continuum of stimulus complexity, with more complex stimuli (e.g., real human bodies) engendering poorer performance, especially when the underlying visuo-spatial representations are damaged or weak. This argument could also apply to the performance of 15-month-olds in the current series of studies: When the body stimuli are relatively simple, schematic images, then 15-month-olds' visuo-spatial knowledge can be recruited to make the scrambled body versus typical body discrimination. However, when the stimuli are complex photographs, their human body knowledge may be overwhelmed by the perceptual and attentional demands of the task.

DeLoache, Pierroutsakos, and Uttal (2003) also make a case for a continuum of stimulus complexity that has developmental implications for performance on various types of tasks. Based on their studies of toddlers' understanding of the nature of external representations, DeLoache and colleagues propose that young children's performance on some cognitive tasks changes as a function of stimulus realism, with more realistic representations (especially three-dimensional models) being harder for toddlers to interpret as representations. We return to this issue in the General Discussion, after we present a series of studies involving typical and scrambled three-dimensional dolls, in the next chapter.

The results of Study 3 suggest that visuo-spatial body representations are intact but relatively weak at 15 months of age. This conclusion derives from data indicating that at 15 months of age, infants' capacity to discriminate scrambled and typical body shapes is influenced by the complexity of the stimuli (they discriminated scrambled from typical human body line drawings but not color photographs), and by task demands (they showed no preference for typical or scrambled body line drawings when presented simultaneously in Slaughter et al., 2002 but did discriminate them in Study 1 in the habituation paradigm). This pattern suggests that detailed visuo-spatial representations of the human body first emerge, perhaps as relatively fragile representations, at 15 months of age.

Study 3 did not replicate the effect of walking that was found in Study 1. In the current study there was no evidence that 12- or 15-month-olds' capacity to discriminate scrambled from typical human bodies was linked to their experience of walking upright. This failure to replicate the effect of motor experience may relate to the issue of stimulus complexity; if the scrambled versus typical body discrimination is easier when the stimuli are schematic line drawings, then the effect of upright sensori-motor experience may be easier to demonstrate in that task compared to the more difficult photograph discrimination task.

STUDY 4: A COMPARISON OF 12-MONTH-OLDS' RESPONSES TO BODIES AND FACES

In Studies 1 and 3, 12-month-olds were insensitive to a transition from typical to scrambled human body shapes. Study 2 established that this insensitivity was not due to 12-month-olds' inability to discriminate two distinct human body images. Thus at 12 months of age, infants do not make a categorical discrimination between scrambled and typical human body shapes, suggesting that they do not have access to a detailed visuo-spatial representation of the human body.

This conclusion contrasts sharply with the data on face perception in infancy, reviewed in Chapter I. When it comes to faces, discrimination of scrambled from typical stimuli is evident in infants as young as a few days old (in visual tracking and preferential looking tasks; Goren et al., 1975; Johnson & Morton, 1991). The apparent difference in developmental trajectories for face and body processing is intriguing. However, the data cannot be directly compared because they involve different experimental techniques. In a previous study, we provided the only direct comparison of face and body visual tasks; in visual preference tasks 12- and 15-month-olds preferred a typical face to a scrambled face, but looked equally long at the typical and scrambled bodies, and 18-month-olds preferred the scrambled body but looked equally long at typical and scrambled faces (Slaughter et al., 2002).

Thus there is some evidence to suggest that visuo-spatial knowledge of the human face develops separately from visuo-spatial knowledge of the whole human form, and it appears that infants' knowledge of faces emerges much earlier in development. Study 4, reported below, directly tests these hypotheses. In this study, 12-month-olds were presented with two habituation conditions: one in which they were habituated to a variety of typical bodies then presented with a scrambled body, and one in which they were habituated to a variety of typical faces then presented with a scrambled face. All stimuli in this study were photographic images, projected on large viewing screens as in Study 3.

Method

Participants

Infants were recruited in a manner identical to that of Study 1. Eighteen infants participated. However, statistical analyses were based on a total of nine 12-month-olds (*M* age, 12 months, 15 days; range, 11 months 20 days to 12 months 25 days; 6 boys, 3 girls), as there was high attrition due to fussiness.

Materials

The body stimuli were a subset of those from Study 3: photographic images of the six typical human bodies, and one scrambled body (the arms extending up from head scrambled body figure (second from left, bottom row Figure 1)), projected onto a screen. This figure was chosen because, as Table 1 shows, across the age groups tested, it was the most salient scrambled body pattern and therefore perhaps the most likely to attract 12-month-olds' attention and engender discrimination in the current study. (It will also been seen in the next chapter that three-dimensional scrambled human body stimuli where the arms extend up from the head are significantly more salient than other three-dimensional scrambled body patterns.)

The typical face stimuli were photographic images depicting six faces of different genders and ages. The scrambled face image was created with Adobe Photoshop software, and had the internal features manipulated to match the configuration of the symmetrical scrambled schematic face used by Goren et al. (1975) and Johnson and Morton (1991). Figure 5 shows the scrambled face photograph used in the study. Note that this design equates the face and body discrimination tasks; both require a categorical discrimination of a scrambled image following habituation to a series of typically configured (face and body) images.

Procedure

The procedure was identical to Study 3 with the following exceptions: Infants were presented with a series of typical body or face images until they reached the habituation criterion, then they were presented with a single scrambled stimulus. Infants' looking to the pictures was measured. Infants were also presented with typical versus scrambled feet and hand images, but the results of these conditions are not presented here. The full procedure lasted approximately five minutes. The order of condition presentation was randomized across infants.

Coding

Coding of data was performed in a manner similar to that of Study 3. Inter-coder reliability on 25% of the data was calculated at 94%. All looking times reported are in milliseconds.

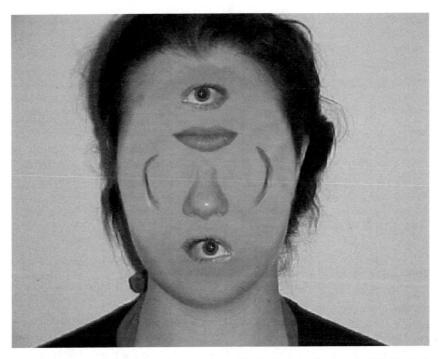

FIGURE 5.—Scrambled face photograph used in the face condition test trial in Study 4.

Results and Discussion

The data from nine infants who did not complete both face and body conditions were omitted. The high attrition rate appeared to be due to the nature of the task, as infants became fussy when required to habituate in a second condition, even though the stimuli were different. The decision was made to maintain a within-subjects design (rather than moving to a between-subjects design) as the study was intended to directly compare dishabituation responses to scrambled faces versus scrambled bodies in the same group of infants.

The mean number of trials to habituation was 9.85 (SD = 1.80) in the face condition and 9.36 (SD = 1.60) in the body condition. To ensure that infants were genuinely habituated, the means for the first three typical face and body trials and the final three typical stimulus trials were compared. For the first three typical face trials, the mean looking time was 8181.44 ms (SD = 3160.89 ms) and for the final three typical face trials the mean looking time was 5679.28 ms (SD = 3396.41 ms). For the first three typical body trials the mean looking time was 6486.49 ms (SD = 3400.12 ms) and for the final three typical body trials the mean looking time was 3546.82 ms (SD = 2415.95 ms). These data confirm that infants met the habituation criterion of 50% decrement in looking to the typical image in both conditions, before they were presented with the scrambled image.

To evaluate infants' responses to typical and scrambled faces and bodies, a 2 (gender) × 2 (condition: faces versus bodies) × 2 (stimulus type: typical versus scrambled) mixed model ANOVA was computed, where looking time was the dependent variable and stimulus type was a repeated measure. This analysis revealed a marginally significant effect of condition, $F(1,7) = 4.54$, $p = .07$, $\eta^2 = .39$, that indicated infants looked longer at faces than bodies overall. There was also a significant condition by stimulus type interaction, $F(1,7) = 6.40$, $p < .05$, $\eta^2 = .48$, indicating that looking times across the transition to a scrambled pattern was different for faces versus bodies. Follow up paired t-tests revealed that infants looked significantly longer at the scrambled face than at the final typical face, $t(8) = 3.13, p < .01$, (M, typical face 4337.25 ms, scrambled face 7437.67 ms; SDs = 2004.65 and 3096.67 ms, respectively), but there was no significant change in looking times from the final typical body to the scrambled body, $t(8) = .42$, ns, (M, typical body 3635.80 ms, scrambled body 3175.47 ms; SDs = 3732.90 and 2809.77 ms, respectively).

An examination of individual infants' looking patterns to the typical and scrambled face pictures supported the looking time analyses: that six of the nine infants (67%) looked longer at the scrambled face than the typical face, whereas only two of the nine infants (22%) looked longer at the scrambled body than the typical body. Thus infants noticed the scrambled face, but failed to notice the scrambled body.

The results of this study replicate the findings from Studies 1 and 3 that 12-month-olds do not dishabituate to a scrambled body following habituation to typical bodies. However, in the current study the same infants did dishabituate to a scrambled face following habituation to typical faces. This within-subjects pattern confirms the conclusion that young infants are sensitive to configural changes to human faces, but they do not exhibit the same sensitivity to configural changes to the human body. With respect to the issue of developing visuo-spatial body knowledge, there are two interpretations for this pattern. One possibility is that faces and bodies are represented separately, and the visuo-spatial representation for faces develops earlier, or is innate in a schematic form. This hypothesis is in line with neuroimaging research that has revealed what appear to be dedicated face processing areas in the adult brain that do not respond to other complex patterns (Kanwisher et al., 1997; McCarthy, Puce, Gore, & Allison, 1997). An alternative interpretation is that the face is part of a complete visuo-spatial representation of the body, not a distinct representation, but face processing develops earlier because that element of visuo-spatial body knowledge is acquired in detail prior to that of the rest of the human body. Either of these hypotheses is possible and we return to them in Chapter IV below; the point we wish to highlight here is that this study demonstrates that 12-month-old infants can make a categorical discrimination in our procedure, even one relevant to a human body stimulus (the face). The specificity of infants' failure in the scrambled versus typical body discrimination task therefore means that what 12-month-olds specifically lack, is detailed visuo-spatial knowledge of the whole human form.

STUDY 5: CATEGORICAL DISCRIMINATION OF ABSTRACT HUMAN BODY ANALOGS

Study 4 demonstrated that 12-month-olds categorically discriminated scrambled from typical faces, while at the same time failing to make a similar discrimination for the whole human body. The purpose of Study 5 was to further test the specificity of young infants' responses to human bodies, by exploring their responses to abstract forms that could be manipulated to create human body analogs.[4]

In Studies 1 and 3, it was established that 18-month olds discriminated scrambled from typical human body shapes. These data indicate that older infants have, or can form on-line, a visuo-spatial representation of the human body that specifies the typical spatial layout of the body, its parts relative to each other and to the whole. This representation allows infants to discriminate scrambled from typical human body shapes. One-year-olds, on the other hand, apparently do not have access to such a representation, as they repeatedly failed to discriminate scrambled from typical human body shapes. Study 4 established that 12-month-olds can nevertheless make a categorical discrimination, between scrambled and typical faces, further indicating that it is specifically a detailed visuo-spatial body representation that is unavailable to infants at 12 months of age. Study 5 was designed to explore 12-month-olds' responses to abstract patterns that were designed to be analogous to human body shapes, in order to explore further the specificity of human body knowledge. For this study we created a series of completely novel geometric forms that we dubbed "geobodies." These pictures consisted of a central geometric "body" with four geometric "limbs" and a "head" that could articulate from the "body" as if on joints (see Figure 6). A series of geobodies in different "postures" was presented, then three scrambled geobodies were shown in the standard experimental design used in the previous studies. This test was designed to reveal what type of knowledge, and what cognitive processes, young infants bring to the human body experiments. We reasoned that if 12-month-olds failed the human body discrimination tasks of Studies 1, 3, and 4 because they are

FIGURE 6.—Six "typical" geobodies (in the top two rows) and three "scrambled" geobodies (in the bottom row) used in Study 5.

incapable of analyzing complex patterns similar to human body shapes (e.g., with a number of articulating parts) then they should fail the "geobodies" discrimination task because it requires a similar visual analysis. However, if 12-month-olds succeed in the "geobodies" discrimination task, then it would indicate that a different cognitive process is engaged when infants are presented with human body shapes as opposed to novel geometric patterns.

Method

Participants

Infants were recruited in a manner identical to that of Study 1. There were 14 infants ranging in age from 11 months 10 days to 12 months 10 days, mean age 11 months 30 days. There were five boys and nine girls.

Materials

The stimuli consisted of nine pictures of brightly colored three-dimensional geometric shapes ("geobodies"), constructed for the purposes of this research. Each shape consisted of a large cylindrical red "torso," two medium-sized blue cylindrical "legs," two small green cylindrical "arms," and a yellow square "head." Pictures were presented on white paper (30 cm × 21.5 cm). The typical geobodies were presented in a variety of configurations, with the following constraints: the large red torso and the yellow head stayed fixed, whereas the blue and green arms and legs articulated at differing angles from the torso so that the overall shapes changed configuration in a manner analogous to the postural changes of the typical human body stimuli used in previous studies (e.g., arms extended up versus out versus down from the torso in different postures). Three scrambled geobodies were constructed for the test phase, each of which violated the standard configuration of the typical geobodies by moving the "arms" and "legs" to different locations on the figure. Figure 6 shows the six typical geobodies and the three scrambled geobodies used in the study.

Pictures were presented to the infant using the viewing screen described in Study 1. A halogen lamp was positioned directly below the picture, pointed upwards, to create a spotlight effect on the pictures. This was found to be necessary because pilot testing indicated that 12-month-olds were loathe to sit through this task, but spotlighting the pictures increased their attention to the images. A hole in the middle of the screen allowed video recording of the infant's looking behavior.

Procedure

The procedure was identical to Study 1 with some minor changes. The looking trials were eight seconds long to minimize attrition. The infant control habituation method was used as in previous studies and as before habituation was defined as a 50% decrement of looking from the first three trials (averaged) to a subsequent three trials. Once habituation to typical geobodies had occurred, the three scrambled geobody pictures were presented individually on consecutive trials. Typical geobody pictures were presented in a fixed order across infants. The order of presentation of scrambled geobodies was counterbalanced across infants with a partial Latin Square. The entire session lasted approximately 5 minutes.

Coding

Infants' looking across all trials was timed and a naive viewer recoded 100% of trials (again, because the looking times were very short in this procedure, we did full reliability coding to ensure accuracy). The inter-coder reliability was 90% and as before, values were taken from the looking times recorded by the first observer. All looking times reported are in milliseconds.

Results and Discussion

The mean number of trials to habituation was 7.86 ($SD = 1.92$). To ensure that infants were genuinely habituated, the means for the first three typical geobody trials and the final three typical geobody trials were compared. For the first three typical trials the mean looking time was 4461.73 ms ($SD = 1495.21$ ms) and for the final three typical trials the mean looking time was 2999.89 ms ($SD = 984.49$ ms). These data confirm that infants met the habituation criterion of 50% decrement in looking to the typical geobodies before they were presented with the scrambled geobodies.

To test whether infants dishabituated upon presentation of the scrambled geobodies, a 2 (gender) × 2 (geobody type: typical geobodies versus scrambled geobodies) mixed model ANOVA was computed, where body type was the repeated measure. The dependent variable was looking time averaged over the last three typical geobody trials and the first three scrambled geobody trials. This analysis revealed a significant main effect for geobody type, $F(1,12) = 8.02$, $p < .02$, $\eta^2 = .40$), that indicated significantly longer looking times for the scrambled geobodies than the typical geobodies (M last three typical geobodies 2999.89 ms, M first three scrambled geobodies 3594.21 ms; $SD = 984.49$ and 1257.64 ms, respectively). No other main effects or interactions were significant. These data show that 12-month-olds were capable of discriminating scrambled from typical geobody shapes, despite typically failing a similar discrimination task for human body shapes (in Studies 1, 3 and 4).[5]

Next the less conservative discrimination analysis was performed by comparing infants' looking at the final typical geobody picture versus the first scrambled geobody picture. A 2 (gender) × 2 (geobody type: final typical vs. first scrambled) mixed model ANOVA was computed, where body type was a repeated measure and looking time was the dependent variable. Results again revealed a significant main effect for geobody type ($F(1,12) = 5.12$, $p < .05$, $\eta^2 = .30$), indicating significantly longer looking times for the first scrambled geobody compared to the final typical geobody ($M = 3496.14$ ms, 2709.00 ms; $SD = 1699.74$ and 1462.17 ms). No other main effects or interactions were significant. Again, this pattern shows that infants were sensitive to the transition from typical to scrambled geobodies. Thus 12-month-olds noticed when the "limbs" of a nonsense geometrical figure were moved from their pre-established cannonical locations, even though infants of that age in the previous studies did not notice a similar change applied to human bodies.

An examination of individual infants' looking patterns to the typical and scrambled body line drawings revealed that 6 of the 14 infants (43%) looked longer at the first scrambled geobody picture than the final typical geobody picture. This pattern suggests that the geobodies discrimination is not especially robust, but given that these were nonsense figures and looking times were relatively short, it is perhaps not surprising that only a minority of infants met our criterion for noticing the transition from typical to scrambled geobody shapes.

The results of this study suggest that different representations or processes underlie infants' performance in the human body and geobody discrimination tasks. In this study, 12-month-olds made a categorical discrimination between scrambled versus typical geobodies, even though the same age infants (and indeed, the very same sample of 12-month-olds; see Footnote 5) failed to make the same discrimination for human bodies in all our previous studies. What accounts for this difference in performance across the two similar discrimination tasks? In both tasks, infants were required to visually analyze a series of typical shapes, and then take note when the typical shapes were scrambled. This was achieved in the geobodies task, but not in the human body task. We suggest that the difference has to do with the knowledge that infants bring to each procedure. When presented with the geobodies task, infants viewed the patterns from a naïve perspective, and accordingly constructed a mental representation of the typical shape of geobodies during the familiarization trials. In the human body task, in contrast, we believe that infants came into the experiment with pre-established knowledge about the human body shape, and that led them to classify all the bodies, including the scrambled ones, as being members of the same category. We propose that this pre-established knowledge was in the form of a schematic visuo-spatial human body representation that was inclusive enough to allow categorization of typical and scrambled bodies as being similar. In this we support Quinn and Eimas' (1998) hypothesis that infants' early representation of humans, (in our terms, the visuo-spatial human body representation), originates as a broad, inclusive pattern characterized by a head on top of an elongated, symmetrical body. With such a human body representation in mind, 12-month-olds may have failed the human body discrimination task because all the bodies, both typical and scrambled, conformed to this pattern. We return to this hypothesis and elaborate on it in the final chapter.

SUMMARY

The results across the five studies in this chapter paint a clear picture of the development of infants' developing visuo-spatial body knowledge, reflected in their responses to typical and scrambled human bodies. At twelve months, infants showed little discrimination of scrambled from typical human bodies (Studies 1, 3 and 4). This insensitivity was not due to (a) an inability to discriminate between different human body pictures (as shown in Study 2 when 12-month-olds discriminated between two individual human body pictures), or (b) to an inability to discriminate scrambled from typical images in general (as shown in Studies 4 and 5 when they discriminated scrambled from typical human faces, and scrambled versus typical abstract geobodies, but not human body shapes). Thus at 12 months, detailed knowledge of the spatial layout of the human body is apparently not yet available to infants.

In contrast to 12-month-olds, 18-month-old infants reliably discriminated scrambled from typical human bodies (Studies 1 and 3). At 15 months of age, infants showed a fragile capacity for discriminating scrambled from typical human bodies; they discriminated scrambled from typical bodies when the stimuli were schematic line drawings (Study 1), but failed to similarly discriminate human body photographs (Study 3). Taken together, these studies indicate that detailed visuo-spatial knowledge of the human body begins to emerge between 15 and 18 months of age. Before that age, we suggest that infants possess a highly schematic, inclusive representation of the spatial attributes of the human body, that leads them to treat scrambled and typical human body shapes as being categorically similar. This conclusion is bolstered by the fact that when presented with abstract geobodies in Study 5, 12-month-olds discriminated scrambled from typical shapes, presumably because the geobodies were unfamiliar and therefore subject to naïve perceptual categorization processes. Categorization of human body shapes, on the other hand, appeared to be influenced by pre-existing knowledge; what we propose is a highly inclusive, schematic visuo-spatial human body representation.

The foregoing visual habituation studies lead to the conclusion that visuo-spatial knowledge of human bodies is first evident sometime between 15 and 18 months of age in normal infants. In the next chapter, we seek to further support and refine this conclusion by carrying out a series of studies using a different experimental paradigm, the object exploration technique, in which infants are presented with typical and scrambled three-dimensional human body shapes.

NOTES

2. Bertenthal, Haith, and Campos (1983) introduced the partial lag design to address the potential problem of spontaneous regression in the infant control procedure. They note that "chance habituators" show a certain amount of pseudo-response recovery to the familiar

stimulus even after the habituation criterion is reached, whereas infants who demonstrate true habituation will have a response curve that remains flat.

The partial lag design controls for chance recovery of interest by introducing a lag condition in which half of the infants are presented with two additional familiarization trials (lag trials) after reaching the habituation criterion. Following the two lag trials, infants are presented with the novel stimulus. The other half of the infants (the nonlag group) are presented with the novel stimulus immediately after they reach the habituation criterion. Looking times on the last two familiarization trials and the first two test trials are compared across groups to assess genuine recovery of interest (in the nonlag group) versus chance recovery of interest (in the lag group; Bertenthal et al., 1983).

While we recognized the value of using a partial lag design in visual habituation studies like those presented in Chapter 2, we chose not to adopt the technique, mainly because the current studies involved testing infants that were relatively old to be enduring a habituation procedure (12- to 18-month-old infants). Pilot testing indicated that infants in this age range became quite restless towards the end of the habituation phase, and it was sometimes difficult for infants to complete the entire experiment. For this reason, it was considered too high a risk to include two additional habituation (lag) trials, for fear of substantially increasing attrition rates.

As the infants' looking times were coded on line (and therefore subject to greater error than post-experimental coding), if there was any ambiguity that the habituation criterion may not have been met while the experiment was in progress, the infant received additional habituation trials. While this increased the chances of attrition, it was thought to be the best option since infants who did not reach habituation criterion would not provide interpretable data. Therefore, a small percentage of infants received the equivalent of lag trials uninten-tionally. Of the infants who received lag trials and completed the experiment, examination of their looking times revealed flat response curves over these "lag" trials, indicating genuine habituation.

Additionally, we have had the opportunity to observe the behavior of infants ranging in age from 6 to 18 months in this experimental paradigm. These observations revealed age-related changes in looking behavior during habituation. On average, infants 12 months and older (like those in the studies reported in Chapter 2) tended to become bored with the familiarization stimuli rapidly and looking times decreased steadily during the familiariza-tion phase. In contrast, younger infants (6- and 9-month-olds) tended to respond more sporadically during the habituation phase, with looking times fluctuating slightly (decreasing and increasing) until they eventually declined and the habituation criterion was reached. Thus, the partial lag design may be important in controlling for spontaneous regression in younger infants' looking times; but it appears that the looking behavior of older infants can be accurately assessed with a standard serial habituation procedure like that used in the Chapter 2 studies.

3. We are indebted to an anonymous reviewer for suggesting this study.

4. We thank Thomas Suddendorf for his creative input to the design of this study.

5. In fact, a subset ($n = 12$) of the 12-month-old infants who successfully discriminated scrambled from typical geobodies in Study 5 was also subsequently presented with a human body discrimination task similar to that reported in Study 3 (this was a control condition for work not reported in this monograph, in which typical and scrambled body photographs were used). Examination of those data revealed that the infants failed to make the scrambled versus typical body discrimination, replicating the 12-month-old results from Studies 3 and 4.

III. OBJECT EXPLORATION STUDIES: INFANTS' DISCRIMINATION OF TYPICAL AND SCRAMBLED DOLLS

A number of recent authors have questioned the wisdom of inferring underlying cognitive representations and processes from infants' performance in visual paradigms alone (Bremner, 2000; Haith, 1998; Langer, Gillette, & Arriaga, 2003; Simon, 1997). One concern is that visual discrimination studies do not engage infants' representational knowledge, but require only low-level, on-line perceptual and attentional processes. For some programs of research, this concern raises serious doubts about data interpretation (see Haith & Benson, 1998 for detailed discussion). As noted in Chapter I, Mandler (1997, 2000) argues that independent cognitive processes are revealed by experimental tasks that require infants to make visual and manual responses. She proposes that visual tasks assess perceptual categorization, a process based on surface properties like shape and texture, whereas manual tasks additionally reveal conceptual categorization, that is "based on what objects do" (Mandler, 2000; p. 3).

In this *Monograph*, we specifically investigate the development of visuo-spatial representations of the human body. These representations are arguably purely perceptual, as they specify information about the spatial layout of the human body, its parts in relation to each other and in relation to the whole form. With this as our target level of knowledge, we propose that inferring infants' visuo-spatial human body knowledge from visual paradigms alone, like those reported in Chapter II, would be reasonable. What we are investigating, in Mandler's terms, is perceptual categorization. However, as reviewed in Chapter I, human body knowledge is known to be represented at several different levels in the brain, and these levels of knowledge interact in some contexts (e.g., Reed & Farah, 1995). It seems likely that at some stage in development, the issues of what bodies look like (represented by visuo-spatial knowledge), and what bodies do (represented by sensori-motor and/or lexical–semantic knowledge) become intertwined. While we are not yet at the stage of investigating how levels of human body knowledge interact in development, we nevertheless chose to extend our study of the development of visuo-spatial body knowledge to include a series of manual habituation studies, reported below. The basic logic of the manual studies is the same as in the previous chapter: We present infants with the opportunity to discriminate scrambled from typical bodies. The extension of this technique to a manual paradigm accomplishes two things. First, it allows us to engage infants in the task more thoroughly than in the visual studies. As mentioned previously 12- to 18-month-olds are relatively old to participate in visual habituation studies and in many of the looking trials in the Chapter II studies, infants were engaged with the stimuli for as few as 5 s or less. Manual tasks are inherently more interesting because they allow infants to freely manipulate the stimuli, so extension of our investigation to include manual tasks allows us to ensure that our pattern of findings, as robust as they were across studies in Chapter II, was not due to artifacts of the visual procedure. Second, the addition of manual tasks also allows us to further address the issue of how the realism of a given stimulus may interact with infants' knowledge. As noted above, DeLoache (1995) and colleagues (DeLoache et al., 2003; DeLoache & Smith, 1999) have argued that some representations are easier for infants and toddlers to process than others. In line with this argument, the studies of Chapter II revealed an apparent stimulus realism effect such that 15-month-olds' capacity to discriminate scrambled from typical human bodies was disrupted when the stimuli were relatively realistic human body photographs. This issue of stimulus realism can be further explored with comparison of performance in visual (involving two-dimensional images) and manual (involving three-dimensional dolls) discrimination tasks.

The following studies used a standard object examination paradigm in which the typical and scrambled body stimuli were dolls of various sizes that infants were allowed to explore and manipulate. The procedure in these studies was as follows: Infants were presented with a fixed number of typical doll experimental trials to establish familiarization to the typical human body shape, then a scrambled test doll was presented. Whereas the Chapter II studies used an infant-controlled procedure in which habituation was calculated on-line in the course of the experiment, the studies reported below presented infants with a fixed number of trials, and habituation was tested after the fact. The main reason for this change was that it was too difficult to code infants' manipulative behavior of the dolls on-line. However, it can be argued that this change in procedure adds additional breadth to our project of exploring infants' human body knowledge across different experimental paradigms.

In these studies, analyses focused on (a) infants' examination of the typical dolls on familiarization trials and (b) infants' recovery of interest (reflected in an increase in examination time) to scrambled dolls on the test trials. We also performed nonparametric analyses using the same criterion for noticing as was used in the Chapter II studies: Infants were classified as

59

noticing the scrambled doll if their examination times increased by a value that exceeded the standard deviation of examination on the final three familiarization trials.

STUDY 6: CATEGORICAL DISCRIMINATION OF THREE-DIMENSIONAL HUMAN BODY SHAPES

The purpose of this study was to further explore the development of visuo-spatial human body knowledge, by testing infants' responses to typical and scrambled dolls. Three scrambled body shapes were created for these studies, loosely based on the scrambled human body pictures used in Chapter II. These were (a) arms raised above the head but attached at the temples, referred to as the "arms on head doll," (b) arms hanging by sides but attached at hips, referred to as the "arms on hips doll," and (c) arms removed completely, referred to as the "armless doll." The armless doll was not "scrambled" in the strict sense that some body parts were moved to non-canonical locations, but for ease of reference all three test dolls are referred to as "scrambled." The choice of these three shapes was largely determined by the physical characteristics of the dolls themselves, which were made of hard plastic that was not easily manipulated.

On the basis of the pattern of data from the Chapter II studies, it was predicted that infants older than 12 months would discriminate scrambled from typical body shapes by showing a recovery of interest upon presentation of the scrambled dolls, following habituation to typical dolls. This pattern would further support the conclusion that a detailed visuo-spatial representation of the human body emerges in the second year of life.

Based on the stimulus realism effect found in Studies 1 versus 3, and also based on the work of DeLoache and colleagues, we expected that the scrambled body discrimination task involving three-dimensional stimuli might be more difficult than the task involving two-dimensional body pictures. Further, previous work has established that manual categorization tasks tend to be more difficult than visual tasks (Younger & Furrer, 2003). Based on these observations, we decided to include a group of 24-month-olds in Study 6, to ensure that at least one age group would demonstrate perfect or nearly perfect performance on the scrambled body discrimination task.

Method

Participants

Infants were recruited in a manner identical to that of Study 1. Statistical analyses were based on a total of 21 12-month-old infants

(M age = 11 months and 30 days: range 11 months 16 days to 12 months 14 days; 9 boys, 12 girls), 20 15-month-olds (M age = 15 months and 8 days: range 14 months 29 days to 15 months 20 days; 10 boys, 10 girls), 19 18-month-olds (M age = 17 months and 29 days: range 17 months 18 days to 18 months 12 days; 10 boys, 9 girls) and 18 24-month-olds (M age = 24 months and 5 days: range 23 months 17 days to 24 months 14 days; 10 boys, 8 girls). An additional two 12-month-olds, four 15-month-olds, four 18-month-olds and two 24-month-olds were tested but excluded from the final sample due to excessive fussiness or experimenter error. In the studies reported in this chapter, fussiness was behaviorally defined as inconsolable crying and/or refusal to look at or touch the dolls on three consecutive trials and/or throwing dolls off the testing table immediately after presentation on three consecutive trials.

Materials

The stimuli consisted of 13 human figures and one bowling pin (see Figure 7 for the dolls used in the study). The human figures represented humans of different ages (babies, adults), sizes (range: 6.5–24 cm); and

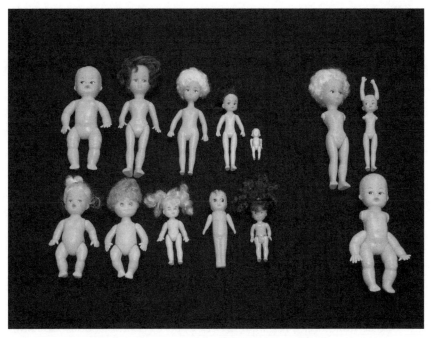

FIGURE 7.—Typical and scrambled dolls used in Studies 6 and 7.

statures (slim, normal), thus variability was quite high. Ten of the dolls were normally shaped, and three were scrambled as described above. All of the dolls were made of hard plastic (excluding the dolls' hair) and were presented naked. The bowling pin was made of yellow plastic and was 25 cm in height.

Procedure

The infant was seated in an infant seat at a table, across from the experimenter. The mother sat on the left of the infant, and a video camera was positioned to the right. Each object was hidden until the experimenter gave it to the infant. Individual trials began with the experimenter placing an object on the table directly in front of the infant and saying, "look what I've got" or "look at this." As soon as the object became visible to the infant, the experimenter began timing the 20 s trial. Infants were allowed to handle and manipulate the objects freely. When the trial ended the experimenter removed the object and immediately presented the next one, beginning the next trial. On occasion, infants firmly pushed the object away, showing signs of boredom, and in this instance the object was removed before the full 20 s had lapsed.

During familiarization, each infant was presented with a total of 10 different dolls, in random order across shape conditions and infants. On the test trial, one scrambled doll was presented and again the infant was allowed to visually and manually explore it. The test trial continued until the infant firmly pushed the doll away or when 35 s had passed. Maximum examination time was set at 35 s for the test trial to avoid the possibility of ceiling effects. There was no risk of artificially inflating dishabituation time from trial 10 to the test trial (due to 20 s habituation trials and 35 s test trials) as no infant was anywhere near reaching ceiling (20 s) on the last habituation trial. If an object was thrown onto the floor at any time during the procedure, it was picked up as quickly as possible and placed back on the table.

Once the 11 doll trials were completed (10 familiarization trials with typical dolls and one scrambled doll test trial), a novel object (the bowling pin) was presented for 30 s. This gave infants a break from dolls before the next series of dolls was presented.

The doll familiarization-test procedure was repeated twice more. Each presentation involved a new random ordering of the same set of typical dolls, and a different scrambled doll on the test trial. Thus each infant participated in three scrambled doll conditions, in which they were familiarized with the series of typical dolls, then shown a novel scrambled doll to test for discrimination. Presentation order of the scrambled dolls was counterbalanced across infants. The entire session lasted approximately 10 min.

Coding

Examination time was the dependent variable in these studies, analogous to looking time in the visual habituation studies. Examination was defined as focused looking or concentration on the object in either the presence or absence of manipulation (Mandler & McDonough, 1993; Oakes, Madole & Cohen, 1991). This definition of examination excluded activities like mouthing and banging. Sessions were videotaped and coded by two independent observers, the second coder being naïve to the hypothesis under investigation. Twenty-five percent of the data were coded by a naïve observer to establish reliability; agreement between the two coders was 91%. For statistical analysis, values were taken from the examination times recorded by the first observer. All examination times reported are in milliseconds.

Results and Discussion

To establish that infants habituated to the typical dolls presented during familiarization, ANOVAs were conducted on infants' looking times across habituation trials. The studies reported in Chapter II did not require statistical analyses to establish habituation as the infant control procedure ensured that each infant was presented with the exact number of trials required for habituation (as the reported means indicated). Because the object exploration procedure was conducted with a fixed number of familiarization trials (corresponding to the number of unique typical body dolls), it was necessary to statistically establish that infants habituated to the typical body shapes.

Two mean-scores were computed: block A refers to mean examination during the first five trials on which typical bodies were presented, and block B refers to mean examination time during the final five typical body examination trials. These were collapsed across the three scrambled doll conditions. A 4 (age: 12, 15, 18 and 24 months) × 2 (blocks: block A vs. block B) × 3 (order: first, second or third presentation) mixed-model ANOVA was computed on examination time to investigate the extent to which infants in the different age groups habituated from block A to block B. The ANOVA revealed a significant main effect of age, $F(3,74) = 6.46$, $p < .01$, $\eta^2 = .21$, reflecting the fact that older infants examined the dolls longer in general. A main effect of block was also found, $F(1,74) = 110.48$, $p < .01$, $\eta^2 = .60$, indicating that examination times declined overall from block A to block B. There was no effect of presentation order, indicating that the pattern of declining interest in the typical dolls was similar across the three consecutive scrambled doll conditions. A significant age × block interaction was also found, $F(3,74) = 3.74$, $p < .05$, $\eta^2 = .13$ indicating that the decline in examination of the dolls from block A to block B varied as a function of age. The age by block interaction was followed up with a series of paired t-tests comparing examination times on block A to block B examination times, separately for each age group. This analysis revealed that at all ages, there was a significant decline in examination times from block A to block B, all $t > 3.17$, all $p < .01$. Thus infants in all four age groups habituated to the typical body dolls prior to presentation of the scrambled dolls.

Two different procedures for analyzing infants' responses to the scrambled dolls were considered: (a) conducting a repeated measures ANOVA between the trial 10 examination time and the test trial examination time (similar to the analyses conducted on visual dishabituation in the Chapter II studies), or (b) subtracting the trial 10 examination time from the test trial to create a difference score. Both methods of analyses are appropriate; the difference score method was selected. The reasons for this choice were as follows: Main effects (overall age differences, unqualified differences in examination times across trials) were not of primary interest, power was sufficient, and because this study included an additional factor of scrambled body shape (e.g., arms on head doll, arms on hips doll, armless doll), difference scores provided a simpler conceptualization of the results. Thus, a difference score for each infant in each condition was created by subtracting the trial 10 examination time from the test trial examination time, thereby representing the magnitude of infants' recovery of interest to the scrambled body shape. This difference in looking time was termed *dishabituation*, and served as the dependent variable in the main analyses.

Results of a 2 (gender) × 4 (age group: 12, 15, 18 and 24 months) × 3 (scrambled body shape: arms on head, arms on hips, armless) mixed-model ANOVA revealed several significant effects. The main effect of age on dishabituation scores, $F(3,70) = 21.71$, $p < .001$, $\eta^2 = .48$, indicated that dishabituation scores (e.g., recovery of interest to the scrambled dolls) varied across age groups (see Table 2). The significant main effect of scrambled doll shape on dishabituation scores, $F(2,140) = 17.76$, $p < .001$, $\eta^2 = .19$, indicated that infants recovered interest more strongly to some of the scrambled dolls compared to the others. There was also a marginally significant main effect of gender, $F(1,70) = 3.49$, $p < .062$, $\eta^2 = .05$ indicating that girls' dishabituation to the scrambled dolls was greater than that of boys.

Finally, there was a marginally significant interaction of scrambled doll shape by age, $F(6,140) = 2.07$, $p < .061$, $\eta^2 = .08$, which indicated that infants' recovery of interest to the three different scrambled doll shapes varied by age group. Since the purpose of this study was to investigate the development of visuo-spatial knowledge of the human body, this marginal interaction was followed up to establish which scrambled dolls were salient to infants of different ages. Follow-up t-tests compared the differences in examination times between trial 10 (the final typical doll) and the test trial

TABLE 2

MEAN EXAMINATION TIMES IN MILLISECONDS (STANDARD DEVIATIONS IN PARENTHESES) FOR
TRIAL 10 AND TEST FOR EACH SCRAMBLED SHAPE BY AGE GROUP IN STUDY 6

Age	Scrambled shape	Mean (SD) for Trial 10 (ms)	Mean (SD) for Test (ms)
24-month-olds	Arms on head	6354.21 (5211.12)	18440.21 (11138.12)
	Armless	6235.45 (5361.21)	13235.12 (10360.01)
	Arms on hips	3791.21 (3060.12)	8611.54 (7550.21)
18-month-olds	Arms on head	3551.21 (3091.12)	11021.75 (10340.10)
	Armless	3342.12 (3441.21)	3892.82 (3411.09)
	Arms on hips	2511.21 (2632.01)	3423.21 (3752.14)
15-month-olds	Arms on head	3333.12 (2355.12)	6963.53 (5251.05)
	Armless	4571.54 (4261.21)	3731.42 (3578.94)
	Arms on hips	4385.12 (2841.21)	4754.12 (3518.70)
12-month-olds	Arms on head	4855.12 (2652.12)	5911.12 (3467.12)
	Armless	3521.21 (1624.12)	2703.62 (1534.12)
	Arms on hips	3847.12 (3511.21)	3932.12 (401.13)

(the scrambled doll) by scrambled doll condition in each age group. These analyses revealed that for the 24-month-old infants there was a significant recovery of interest to all three scrambled doll shapes, all t's(17) > 2.78, p's < .01, such that examination time in the test trials were significantly greater than examination times in the final typical doll familiarization trials. Paired t-tests showed that 18-month-old infants dishabituated from trial 10 to test only in response to the arms on head doll, $t(18) = 3.45$, $p < .01$, but not for the armless doll, $t(18) = 1.72$, ns, or the arms on hips doll, $t(18) = 1.78$, ns. Similarly, paired t-tests indicated that 15-month-old infants dishabituated from trial 10 to test only for the arms on head doll, $t(19) = 3.82$, $p < .01$, but not for the armless doll ($t(19) = .99$, ns), or the arms on hips doll ($t(19) = .55$, ns). There was no significant difference between trial 10 and test for the 12-month-olds in any of the scrambled doll conditions, all t's < 1.57, ns, indicating that there was no significant dishabituation to the scrambled dolls in the youngest age group.

Figure 8 portrays the mean examination times, collapsed across scrambled body shape condition, on each trial by age group. This graph shows that recovery of interest in the scrambled dolls increased with age, but as the preceding t-tests revealed (see also Table 2), the 15- and 18-month-olds showed recovery of interest only to the arms on head doll. The particular salience of the arms on head scrambled body shape is also reflected in Table 1 where dishabituation to the arms raised from head human body line drawing was most pronounced. Again, this pattern indicates that some

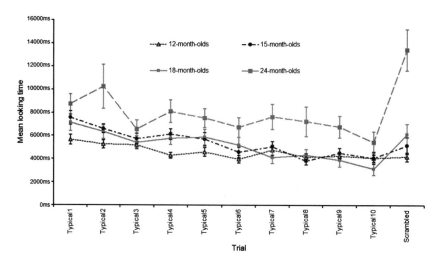

FIGURE 8.—Mean examination times for the typical and scrambled dolls (collapsed across scrambled body shape) by age group in Study 6.

human body shape violations are more obvious than others; however it appears that by 24 months of age, infants' visuo-spatial body knowledge is sufficiently developed such that they were sensitive to all of the scrambled dolls presented.

The nonparametric analyses confirmed these patterns. An examination of individual infants' looking patterns to the typical and scrambled dolls revealed that of the 12-month-old infants, seven of the 21 (33%) looked longer at the arms on head doll than the last typical doll presented, three of the 21 infants (14%) noticed the armless doll, and five of the 21 infants (24%) noticed the arms on hips doll. Among the 15-month-olds, 14 of the 20 (70%) looked longer at the arms on head doll compared to the last normal doll presented, four of the 20 infants (20%) noticed the armless doll and four of the 20 infants (20%) noticed the arms on hips dolls. Of the 18-month-old infants, 15 of the 19 (79%) noticed the arms on head doll, three of the 19 infants (16%) noticed the armless doll and five of the 19 infants (26%) noticed the arms on hips doll. Finally, of 24-month-old infants, 16 of the 18 (89%) noticed the arms on head doll, 14 of the 18 infants (78%) noticed the armless doll and 10 of the 18 infants (56%) looked longer at the arms on hips doll than the last typical doll presented. This pattern again shows that the youngest infants in this study did not notice any of the three scrambled body shapes presented in the test trials, while 15- and 18-month-olds noticed only the arms on head body shape violation. By 24 months, most infants noticed all violations of the human body shape.

Next, 12-month-olds' dishabituation scores were analyzed with respect to their status as walkers, as was done in Study 1. Walking status was unfortunately not recorded for three of the infants. A one-way ANOVA with walking (yes, [$n = 10$] or no [$n = 8$]) as the between-subjects factor was computed on the 12-month-olds' dishabituation scores, collapsed across scrambled body type. No significant effect of walking on infants' dishabituation to the scrambled dolls was found, $F(1,17) = .74, \eta^2 = .04$, ns. This failure to find a walking effect was also evident in Study 3 and suggests two interpretations: It could reflect an interaction of task difficulty with a genuine walking effect, such that it is harder to establish the (perhaps subtle) effect of upright locomotor experience on infants' developing visuo-spatial body knowledge when the task is made difficult for 12-month-olds. This could explain why the walking effect disappeared in Study 3 and in the current study when the human body stimuli were more complex and realistic. Alternatively, the waking effect found in Study 1 could simply be Type I statistical error.

Finally, we tested whether 12-month-old infants' failure to discriminate the typical and scrambled dolls could be explained by a general fatigue effect, brought on by the fixed number of familiarization trials (recall the visual habituation studies were infant-controlled, so that familiarization trials were terminated once infants reached the habituation criterion). To test this possibility, we examined 12-month-olds' responses to the bowling pin that was presented directly after the scrambled doll. A paired t-test comparing examination of the first scrambled doll presented and the bowling pin presented immediately afterwards revealed significantly greater examination for the bowling pin than the scrambled doll ($t(20) = 2.269$ $p < .05$; $M = 5657.33, 4107.42$; $SD = 1855.81$ and 2216.03, respectively). This indicated that 12-month-old infants in this procedure did recover interest to a perceived novel object, meaning that they were not fatigued and therefore unable to respond to novelty in the previous scrambled body trial. A paired t-test comparing examination of the second scrambled doll presented and the second presentation of the bowling pin also revealed significantly greater examination for the bowling pin than the scrambled doll even though by this time the bowling pin was no longer completely novel ($t(20) = 3.529$ $p < .01$; $M = 4102.05, 2314.57$; $SD = 1774.95$ and 1575.10, respectively). Again, this indicates that infants significantly recovered interest to what they perceived as a novel and interesting object (this just happened not to be a scrambled doll). Unfortunately, this analysis was not possible after presentation of the third scrambled doll, as the purpose of presenting the bowling pin was to reduce boredom by interrupting the sequence of dolls so the bowling pin was not presented after the final set of dolls. Overall, these analyses provide evidence that 12-month-old infants' failure to discriminate scrambled from typical dolls was not due to fatigue; when presented with a novel bowling pin, 12-month-olds recovered interest, despite failing to notice the scrambled body doll on the previous trial.

The pattern of results from Study 6 is reasonably consistent with findings from the visual habituation studies reported in Chapter II. Fifteen-month-olds in the visual habituation paradigm showed some sensitivity to scrambled body shapes, and similarly showed limited sensitivity to scrambled bodies in the object examination task. Eighteen-month-olds demonstrated robust discrimination of scrambled body shapes in the visual habituation studies, but like the 15-month-olds, dishabituated only to the arms on head scrambled doll in the object examination task. In the current study, 24-month-olds showed robust discrimination of scrambled from typical body shapes. The age discrepancy for robust discrimination of scrambled from typical body shapes across the visual and manual experimental paradigms was not unexpected, as noted, much previous work has established that infants' categorization abilities appear to vary with the type of task used to assess them. In general, infants make categorical distinctions earlier when tested with visual tasks (visual preference, visual habituation) compared to manual tasks (object examination, sequential touching; Younger & Furrer, 2003; see Mareschal & Quinn, 2001 for a brief review). The reason for this task effect is debated; it may reflect distinct categorization processes as proposed by Mandler (1997, 2000), or it may simply reflect differential sensitivity of visual versus manual paradigms (Younger & Furrer, 2003, Quinn & Eimas, 2000). The point we wish to highlight is that the overall pattern of data from the current study is remarkably consistent with that of the Chapter II studies, with infants' performance on manual categorization tasks reasonably in line with their visual task performance, and data from both types of task indicating that detailed visuo-spatial human body knowledge develops sometime in the second year of life.

STUDY 7: 12-MONTH-OLDS' DISCRIMINATION OF
INDIVIDUAL THREE-DIMENSIONAL HUMAN BODY SHAPES

Studies 1, 3, 4, and 6, using both human body pictures and dolls as stimuli, indicated that 12-month-old infants, unlike their older peers, did not exhibit recovery of attention when presented with scrambled human body shapes following habituation to typical body shapes. This pattern suggested that at 12 months of age, infants do not make a categorical discrimination between scrambled human bodies and typical human bodies, leading to the conclusion that infants younger than 15–18 months do not possess a detailed visuo-spatial human body representation.

In Study 2, it was established that 12 months olds could discriminate two individual typical human body shapes, or two individual scrambled human body shapes. These data supported our conclusions, because they indicated that young infants can make simple perceptual discriminations of different body shape patterns, but what they fail to do is to discriminate between typical and scrambled bodies in general. Study 7 was designed to further test 12-month-old infants' perceptual discrimination of two different body shapes. In Study 7, infants were habituated to a single typical doll then on the test trial they were presented with the highly salient arms on head doll used in Study 6. They were also presented with an abstract human body analog (a variant of the bowling pin figure used in Study 6 manipulated to loosely resemble a body), followed by a "scrambled" version of the bowling pin. The purpose of this study was to evaluate 12-month-olds' capacity to make a simple perceptual discrimination between a typical object (in two conditions: doll and bowling pin) and a scrambled version of the same object. We argue that this is a purely perceptual discrimination because it does not involve generalization; infants simply have to respond to a change in the spatial configuration of individual objects. We hypothesized that 12-month-olds would dishabituate to a scrambled shape following familiarization with an individual typical shape, and that this would be demonstrated in both the human body and bowling pin conditions. Thus this study allowed us to directly test whether infants' perceptual responses to the dolls would be different from their perceptual responses to an abstract shape. If not, then that would suggest that similar perceptual processes were involved in both tasks.

Method

Participants

Infants were recruited in a manner identical to that of Study 1. Statistical analyses were based on a total of 18 12-month-old infants, ranging in age from 11 months 15 days to 12 months 14 days, M age 12 months 4 days. There were 10 boys and eight girls. Five infants were omitted due to not habituating during the familiarization trials.

Materials

A subset of the dolls used in Study 6 was presented; these included one of the typical dolls and the arms on head scrambled doll constructed from an identical typical doll. The yellow plastic bowling pin from Study 6 was manipulated so that the typically shaped bowling pin had four protruding plastic "limbs" extending out from the body. These were constructed from the tops of identical bowling pins such that all four "limbs" were the same color and shape as the top of the bowling pin. The "scrambled" bowling pin had two of the "limbs" moved to the top of the pin, analogous to the arms on head doll scrambled shape.

Procedure

The procedure was identical to that of Study 6 with two exceptions. First, there were four instead of 10 familiarization trials in which the typical shape was presented, to minimize attrition rates. Second, infants were presented with only the one scrambled shape in each of the two conditions (e.g., doll and bowling pin). The entire session lasted no more than five minutes.

Coding

Coding of data was identical to that of Study 6. Reliability was calculated on 25% of the data coded by a naïve observer. Agreement was 89%, and as before values were taken from the examining times recorded by the first observer. All examination times reported are in milliseconds.

Results and Discussion

To ensure that infants habituated, the means for the first two typical body trials (block A) and the final two typical body trials (block B) were compared for both doll and bowling pin conditions. Paired t-tests revealed a significant difference in examination times between block A and block B for the doll, $t(17) = 5.63$, $p < .001$ (M, block A 7258.21 ms, block B 4762.02 ms; $SD = 2924.25$ and 2533.35 ms) and also for the bowling pin, $t(17) = 5.13$, $p < .001$ (M, block A 7095.22 ms, block B 4662.19 ms; $SD = 2572.81$ and 2400.29 ms). These data indicated that in both conditions, examination times in block A were significantly larger than those in block B, thus infants habituated successfully to both the typical doll and the "typical" bowling pin.

To evaluate infants' responses to the introduction of a scrambled shape in both conditions, pre-planned paired t-tests were calculated. These tests showed that in both conditions, there were significant increases in examination times from the final habituation trial to the test trial. For the dolls, $t(17) = 4.68$, $p < .01$; M, final habituation trial 3656.11 ms, test trial 6809.83 ms; $SD = 2265.73$ and 2719.04 ms respectively). For the bowling pins, $t(17) = 5.13$, $p < .01$; M, final habituation trial 4387.33 ms, test trial 7249.33 ms; $SD = 2524.41$ and 3802.46 ms, respectively).

An examination of individual infants' looking patterns to the dolls revealed that 12 of the 18 infants (67%) looked longer at the scrambled doll than the final typical doll. Similarly, 13 of the 18 infants (72%) looked longer at the scrambled bowling pin compared to the final typical bowling pin.

These results indicated that, consistent with Study 2, 12-month-olds discriminated between two individual human body shapes. That is, 12-

month-olds noticed when the human body shape changed, but as Study 6 showed, they did not notice the categorical distinction between typical body shapes and scrambled body shapes. This study also established that 12-month-olds discriminated between two individual nonsense shapes, and their recovery of interest to a configural change in bowling pin shapes was equivalent to their recovery of interest in configural human body changes (mean difference between final familiarization trial and test trial for the doll was 3153.72 ms and for the bowling pin was 2862.00 ms; these differences are not significantly different, $t(18) = .29$, ns). As with Study 5, this suggests that infants were simply responding to the configural changes in the objects; a human body shape violation was no more salient than a change to the spatial properties of a nonsense figure.

The pattern of data indicates that at 12 months, infants are sensitive to featural changes in a single human body exemplar, such that they noticed when an individual doll's body shape was changed, but they do not generalize across exemplars to make the categorical discrimination between scrambled and typical human body shapes. This finding further supports our hypothesis that at 12 months, infants do not yet have access to a detailed visuo-spatial human body representation.

STUDY 8: INFANTS' RESPONSES TO A SCRAMBLED VERSUS A SHAPE-CONTROL DOLL

In Study 6 the investigation of three different violations of the human body shape revealed that the arms on head scrambled doll was more salient than the other two scrambled dolls (armless and arms on hips) for 15-, 18- and 24-month-old infants (with 15- and 18-month-olds dishabituating only to the arms on head scrambled body shape).

There are three explanations for the relative saliency of the arms on head doll. The first is purely perceptual: the arms on head shape may have been particularly salient because the arms extending upward from the head made the whole doll appear longer and larger than the majority of the other dolls. The second relates to infants' expectations about the human head/face: the arms on head scrambling resulted in a violation of the typical shape of the head/face region, and this violation, rather than a violation of the expected body shape, may have captured infants' attention. As Study 4 demonstrated, infants' sensitivity to scrambled faces emerges earlier than sensitivity to scrambled bodies, so the relative salience of the arms on head violation could be related to infants' well-established knowledge about the human face. A final possibility is that the arms on head scrambled doll represents a biologically impossible human body shape (in contrast to the armless doll, which is biologically possible, and the arms on hips doll which appears highly atypical to adults but is closer to being biologically possible than arms on head). Thus infants' earlier-developing sensitivity to the arms on head scrambled doll may have been a matter of general perceptual saliency, violation of expectations about the human face/head shape, or violation of expectations about the human body shape. Study 8 was designed to untangle these three possibilities.

In Study 8, infants were tested in two conditions: a scrambled doll condition and a control condition in which the test doll had a similar, but biologically possible, body shape compared to the scrambled doll. In both conditions infants were habituated to a series of typical dolls, then on the final trial they were presented with the test doll. In the scrambled body condition the test doll was an arms on head scrambled doll similar to the one that was used in Studies 6 and 7. In the control condition, the doll had a typical body shape and its hair was arranged in piggy-tails that were wired to extend upright from the head, creating an overall shape that was identical to the scrambled doll. Thus the control piggy-tail doll was perceptually similar to the scrambled body doll, but it did not represent a violation of the typical human body shape as it still had its arms attached to its shoulders. If infants in Study 6 dishabituated to the arms on head scrambled doll on the basis of perceptual saliency or on the basis of an unexpected face/head shape, then it was predicted that they would dishabituate to the piggy-tail doll equally compared to the scrambled doll. If, on the other hand, infants in Study 6 were sensitive to the violation of the human body shape that the arms on head doll represented, then it was predicted that they would dishabituate more strongly to the scrambled body doll compared to the control doll.

Method

Participants

These included 20 in each age group of 15-month-olds (*M* age = 15 months and 12 days, range 15 months 0 days to 15 months 21 days; 11 boys, 9 girls), 18-month-olds (*M* age = 18 months and 2 days, range 17 months 20 days to 18 months 14 days; 10 boys, 10 girls) and 24-month-olds (*M* age = 24 months and 4 days, range 23 months 14 days to 24 months 14 days; 10 boys, 10 girls). An additional 15-month-old, three 18-month-olds and two 24-month-olds were tested but excluded from the final sample due to excessive fussiness.

Materials

The stimuli consisted of eight dolls plus the bowling pin used in Study 6. The typical dolls were a subset of those used in Study 6; they represented humans of different ages (babies, adults), sizes (range: 16–28 cm); and statures (slim, average). Six typically shaped dolls were used for familiarization, similar to Study 6 (there were fewer familiarization trials included in this study, based on habituation curves established in Study 6, to minimize attrition). The two test dolls were (a) an arms on head scrambled doll and (b) a doll with a typical body shape but whose shape resembled the arms on head doll because its piggy-tails were wired to extend straight up from her head. Figure 9 shows the set of dolls used in this study.

Procedure

All infants completed two testing conditions: scrambled doll and piggy-tail doll. In both conditions infants were presented with six different typical dolls in 20 s familiarization trials. The typical dolls were randomized for order of presentation across condition and across infants. If the infant pushed the doll away or said "no," the doll was removed before 20 s had elapsed. On the test trials (trial 7 in both conditions), one of the test dolls was presented. The test doll was given to the infant until the infant pushed it away or if 35 s had passed. Infants were allowed to explore the dolls freely. If

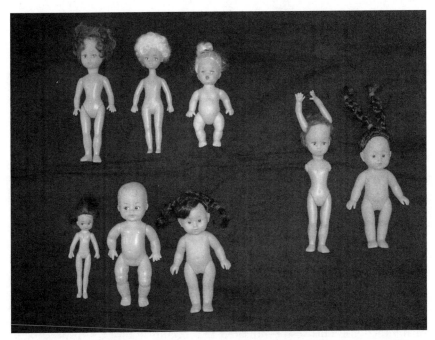

FIGURE 9.—Typical dolls and arms on head and piggy tail test dolls used in Study 8.

a doll was thrown onto the floor, it was retrieved as quickly as possible and placed back on the table.

Upon completion of the first condition, the bowling pin was presented for 30 s to refresh the infants' attention to dolls. Then the second condition was run, in the same manner as the first one. The order of presentation of the scrambled doll and piggy-tail doll conditions was counterbalanced across infants. The entire session lasted approximately 5 min.

Coding

Coding of data was identical to that of Study 1. Reliability coding by a naïve observer was performed on 25% of the data and was calculated at 94%. Examination times are reported in milliseconds.

Results and discussion

To test whether infants habituated to the typical dolls presented during familiarization, two mean-scores were computed: block A refers to mean examination during the three trials where typical bodies were presented, and block B refers to mean examination time during the final three typical body examination trials. A 3 (age: 15, 18, and 24 months) by 2 (blocks: block A vs. block B) mixed-model ANOVA was computed on examination times to investigate the extent to which infants in the different age groups habituated from block A to block B. The ANOVA revealed a significant main effect of age, $F(1,57) = 3.25$, $p < .05$, $\eta^2 = .10$, that indicated older infants examined the dolls longer in general. A main effect of block was also found, $F(1,57) = 20.09$, $p < .001$, $\eta^2 = .26$, indicating that examination times declined from block A to block B. No other main effects or interactions were significant. This analysis indicated that all age groups successfully habituated to the typical body dolls, reflected in the overall decrease in examination times from block A to block B.

Next, we analyzed infants' responses to the scrambled and control test dolls. As in Study 6, a difference score for each infant in each condition was created by subtracting the trial 6 examination time from the test trial examination time, this dishabituation score represented the magnitude of infants' recovery of interest when presented with the test doll.

Results of a 3 (age group: 15-, 18- and 24-month-olds) $\times$ 2 (gender) $\times$ 2 (condition: scrambled versus control) mixed model ANOVA with condition as the repeated measure and dishabituation score as the dependent variable was computed. This analysis revealed a main effect of condition, $F(1,54) = 18.17$, $p < .001$, $\eta^2 = .25$, and no other significant main effects or interactions. This result indicated that infants at all ages dishabituated more strongly to the scrambled body doll compared to the control doll: M

74

dishabituation score for the arms on head doll = 5901.37 ms, and for the control piggy tail doll = 2553.73 ms; SD = 5326.26 and 4291.28 ms, respectively.

Individual infants' looking patterns were similar to the overall pattern of the dishabituation scores. Of 15-month-old infants, 16 of the 20 (80%) noticed the arms on head doll whereas 12 of the 20 infants (60%) noticed the piggy-tail doll. For the 18-month-old infants, 16 of the 20 (80%) noticed the arms on head doll whereas seven of the 20 infants (35%) noticed the piggy-tail doll. Finally, for the 24-month-old infants, 15 of the 20 (75%) looked longer at the arms on head doll compared to the last typical doll presented and 11 of the 20 infants (55%) looked longer at the piggy-tail doll than the last normal doll presented. Thus at each age, a greater number of infants noticed the doll that represented a human body shape violation, than noticed the shape control doll.

The results of this study indicated that infants dishabituated to the scrambled body doll significantly more strongly than to the control doll. The control piggy-tail doll had a similar overall shape compared to the scrambled doll, with the exception that the piggy-tail doll had arms attached at the shoulders. However, since Study 6 demonstrated that 15- and 18-month-olds did not dishabituate to an armless scrambled doll, the presence/absence of arms presumably was not salient to the younger infants in this study.

Thus the piggy-tail doll controlled for perceptual salience (it was equally as long as the scrambled doll) and for violation of the typical head/face shape (it had extensions raising up from the head) but the difference was that the piggy tail doll did not violate the typical human body shape. Fifteen- and 18-month-old infants' may have dishabituated more strongly to the scrambled doll compared to the control doll because even though both dolls had similarly shaped heads (with protrusions extending upwards) the arms on head scrambled doll had obvious flesh-colored arms terminating in recognizable hands extending from her head, while the piggy tail doll had unusual, but obvious and allowable hair in the same location. Thus even though the overall head shape of the two test dolls was similar, the texture and detailed features of the head additions must have been salient to infants. In line with this, Guajardo and Woodward (2002) reported that 9-month-old infants' interpretation of human hands depended on surface qualities like skin color and texture. The fact that infants dishabituated more strongly to the arms on head doll compared to the piggy tail doll indicates that they were more sensitive to a violation of the typical human body shape compared to a change in overall size and shape of the doll, or to a violation of the expected shape of the face/head. Thus the results of this study further support the conclusion that infants of 15–18 months of age have begun to develop a detailed visuo-spatial representation of the human body, evidenced in their principled expectations about the typical human body shape.

SUMMARY

The results of the three studies reported in this chapter add confidence and some complexity to the developmental picture painted in the previous chapter. This series of object examination studies fairly closely replicated the pattern of results established with the visual habituation studies of Chapter II; with the following similarities noted:

(a) 12-month-olds showed no sensitivity to scrambled human body shapes following habituation to typical body shapes (Study 6) and this lack of responsiveness was not due to an inability to make perceptual discriminations between two individual dolls (Study 7).

(b) Infants older than 12 months discriminated between scrambled and typical human body shapes (Study 6) and this discrimination was shown to be significantly stronger than a similar shape discrimination that did not involve an impossible human body shape (Study 8).

The main difference noted between Chapters II and III results was that in the object examination studies, it was not until 24 months of age that infants demonstrated robust discrimination of all types of scrambled bodies from typical bodies, while in the visual habituation studies robust discrimination was apparent by 18 months of age. As noted however and discussed in more detail below, this pattern was not unexpected because previous categorization research has established that categorical discriminations tend to be made in visual paradigms before they are demonstrated in similar manual paradigms. In the big picture, the studies in Chapters II and III reveal remarkable agreement on the early development of visuo-spatial body knowledge: The ability to discriminate scrambled from typical human bodies initially emerges sometime around 15–18 months of age.

IV. DISCUSSION

The foregoing series of studies is the first to systematically address the early development of visuo-spatial human body knowledge. The eight studies reported in Chapters II and III tested infants with two different research methodologies (visual habituation, object exploration) and a variety of human body stimuli (line drawings, photographs, dolls). Across the studies, the results were highly consistent: At 12 months of age infants discriminated two different individual human bodies, but it was not until 15–18 months of age that they began to make a categorical discrimination between typical and scrambled human bodies. In this final chapter, we first discuss some of the methodological issues relevant to interpretation of the data, then explore several conclusions that derive from the results of the studies and outline ideas for further research in this area.

METHODOLOGICAL ISSUES

The pattern of data in the studies of this monograph is highly consistent across the two different experimental paradigms. While infants' discrimination of scrambled from typical bodies was evidenced slightly earlier in the visual habituation studies compared to the object examination studies, a fairly stable developmental trajectory emerges whether we consider infants' preferences for typical and scrambled bodies, infants' looking times in a standard familiarization/dishabituation paradigm, or their responses in an object examination paradigm. Thus the overall conclusion, that detailed visuo-spatial knowledge of the human body develops in the second year of life, is based on multiple studies with multiple experimental techniques. However, even with this experimental variety, there are some methodological issues that need to be considered with respect to the studies presented. Some of these are relevant to infancy research in general, whereas others are specific to this work.

The Representation Problem

It is a standard practice in developmental psychological research to present infants and young children with representations of real-world referents, measure their responses to those representations, and then draw conclusions about infants' knowledge of the referents. In the case of our studies, we have shown infants various types of objects that represent the human body (line drawings, photographs, dolls), and we have drawn conclusions about infants' human body knowledge from their reactions to these stimuli. For instance, we found that 12-month-olds are not surprised when presented with an arms on head scrambled body shape, while 18-month-olds are surprised, and from that pattern of data we have concluded that detailed visuo-spatial human body knowledge does not develop until half-way through the second year of life. This conclusion seems warranted, especially given the range of stimuli we have used across the different studies. However, it remains a possibility that 12-month-olds would express surprise if presented with a real human whose arms grew out of his head. Despite our best efforts (e.g., presenting realistic color photographs in Study 3 and three-dimensional body stimuli in Studies 6 to 8), we cannot rule out the possibility that our pattern of data derives not from young infants' failure to discriminate scrambled from typical human bodies, but instead from their failure to see the line drawings, photographs and dolls that we presented, as representations of humans. This caveat is not specific to our studies, as the majority of categorization research with infants implicitly assumes that infants understand that pictures and toy replicas of objects represent "real" objects in the world.

Do infants treat representations, including drawings, photos and toys, and their real-world referents similarly? Recent studies that have addressed this question indicate that it is sometime between 18 and 24 months of age that infants treat representations and their referents as equivalent (Tomasello, Striano, & Rochat, 1999; Johnson & Furrer, 2004; but see Mandler & McDonough, 1996, 1998 for an opposing view). Particularly relevant to the development of human body knowledge, DeLoache and colleagues recently showed that toddlers are surprisingly poor at matching body parts between real bodies and representations of bodies. In the context of their program of research on the development of representational understanding in toddlers, these investigators presented toddlers with a doll and asked them to put a sticker on the doll's body so that it was in the same place as a sticker placed on their own bodies. Even at age two and a half, toddlers were surprisingly bad at this, failing nearly 50% of the time, though these same toddlers were able to localize the relevant body parts by pointing (DeLoache & Marzolf, 1995). Further research (DeLoache & Smith, 1999) showed that toddlers performed nearly perfectly on similar tasks in which they were asked to map sticker locations from one doll to another, or from one person (an experimenter) to another (themselves). So the problem was in mapping body locations between real bodies and representations of bodies.

If we accept these data as relevant to the studies presented in Chapters II and III, then they lead to the suggestion, discussed above, that infants younger than 18 months may not have discriminated scrambled from typical human body pictures and dolls simply because before that age, infants did not see those human body representations as relating to real humans, and therefore may have not recruited their human body knowledge when responding to the stimuli. However, with respect to the current studies, several points can be made in their defence. As noted previously, DeLoache and colleagues (2003) argue for a continuum of realism among representations, with two-dimensional line drawings being less realistic than color photos or three-dimensional stimuli. They argue that more realistic representations are particularly confusing to young children, who have trouble keeping their representational function in mind when the objects themselves are compelling. This hypothesis could explain our pattern of data across Studies 1 and 3, in which large color photographs of human bodies made it more difficult for infants to discriminate scrambled from typical bodies (recall that 15 month olds discriminated human body line drawings but failed to discriminate the same stimuli when presented as photographs; also the nonparametric analyses showed that a smaller proportion of 18-month-olds noticed the transition to scrambled body shapes when they were photographs as opposed to line drawings). The idea would be that the photograph version of the task was more difficult because the photos were so compelling in themselves, that infants were less likely to recognize or process them as representations of the human body. This interpretation would also suggest that the manual habituation studies should show even later development of the scrambled body–typical body discrimination, given that the dolls are highly compelling, three-dimensional stimuli. This pattern held, but at the same time, there was variation in infants' responses to the specific shapes of the dolls; 15- and 18-month-old infants noticed the arms on head doll, but not the other two scrambled dolls, in Study 6. Thus it is not a straightforward conclusion that more realistic human body stimuli (like three-dimensional dolls) engender poorer performance on the scrambled body discrimination task. The overall pattern of data from Chapters II and III suggests an interaction of the representation problem with developing knowledge, such that the realism of body stimuli influences infants' performance on tasks that reflect human body knowledge. As noted above, this interpretation is also suggested by task performance in adult autotopagnosic patients, who sometimes show stimulus realism effects in body part localization tasks (Felician et al., 2003) but who presumably have no trouble making the link between representations and their referents.

A couple of further points can be made about the representation problem in relation to the studies reported in Chapters II and III. First, in Study 4, we directly compared infants' responses to scrambled bodies versus scrambled faces, and found a clear dissociation. If young infants did not discriminate scrambled from typical bodies because they did not interpret pictures of human bodies as bodies, it is not clear why infants would show a different response pattern when it comes to faces. It could be argued that the "leap" from a face picture to the real thing is shorter than a "leap" from a body picture to the real thing, as face pictures and real faces are closer in size to each other, and perhaps infants have more experience interpreting and identifying pictures of faces. However, if the principle is that infants do not understand representations as such, this exemption for faces seems rather *ad hoc*. Second, Study 5 showed that 12-month-olds' pattern of responding to abstract, meaningless shapes (geobodies) was different from their well-established pattern of responding to human body shapes. That is, in the geobodies task, 12-month-olds categorically discriminated scrambled from typical shapes, whereas in every other study we reported, they failed to make such a categorical discrimination for human body shapes. We proposed that infants were successful on this task because the geobodies were completely novel, and so infants were not influenced by pre-existing knowledge about the shapes. In contrast, we argued that infants failed the human body discrimination task because they came to the procedure with a highly inclusive, schematic visuo-spatial human body representation that led them to categorize scrambled and typical bodies as being similar. This interpretation assumes that infants' responding to the human body stimuli was influenced by their real-world knowledge about the spatial attributes of the human form. If 12-month-old infants saw the human body pictures as meaningless shapes on paper, then they should have demonstrated similar responding to human body pictures and abstract geobody pictures. That was not the case.

Limitations of the Paradigm

While we argue that we have good converging operations in this program of research to date, including visual preference, visual habituation and object examination, recent research and theorizing has made it clear that developmental trends in categorization are closely linked to the experimental paradigm used in testing. Since a number of variables are known to affect infants' looking behavior (complexity, novelty, exposure time; see Hunter, Ames, & Koopman, 1983), altering procedural parameters might change the 15–18-month watershed for discrimination of scrambled from typical bodies found in this series of studies. One of the strengths of the studies in this monograph, we argue, is the use of two distinct research methodologies and the correspondence in results across methods. To further validate the developmental data presented here, future studies of infants' responses to typical and scrambled human bodies should further expand the range of methodologies used, by testing infants with alternative habituation techniques, as well as alternative experimental paradigms such as sequential touching and grouping, match-to-sample tasks, inductive generalization and naming.

One Categorization Process or Two?

Our aim was to explore the development of visuo-spatial human body representations, defined *a priori* as specifying the spatial attributes of the whole human body, its parts in relation to each other and to the whole. Thus our concern was the development of representations that are arguably purely perceptual. We chose to use two distinct methodologies to assess the development of visuo-spatial human body knowledge: visual habituation and object exploration. As reviewed above, Mandler (1997, 2000) has argued that these two experimental paradigms assess two distinct categorization processes: perceptual categorization via visual tasks and conceptual categorization via manual tasks. Because of the nature of the visuo-spatial body representations under study, we have made no claims about perceptual versus conceptual categorization. Mandler's argument would suggest that infants' performance in the visual habituation tasks of Chapter II reflected perceptual categorization, based on what human bodies look like, whereas performance on the object exploration tasks of Chapter III reflected conceptual categorization, based on what human bodies do. We doubt that this is the case, for several reasons.

First, we note that the converging developmental trajectories for performance in our visual and manual tasks suggest that the same representational knowledge was assessed with both types of task. This may simply mean that in the studies reported here, manual tasks assessed perceptual representations (e.g., knowledge about what human bodies look like). This interpretation is in line with our argument that the visuo-spatial body representations under investigation are perceptual in nature (rather than conceptual, in Mandler's terms). We do not discount the idea that two distinct categorization processes may exist in infancy, and even allow that those processes may typically be assessed with different tasks, but we maintain that was not the case in the studies reported in Chapters II and III.

It might still be argued that the studies reported in Chapters II and III reflect distinct perceptual and conceptual categorization processes that happen to converge in development, leading to the developmental synchrony we observed. Given that many authors consider that sensorimotor, visuo-spatial and lexical–semantic body representations are likely to interact, it could be argued from this perspective that what our results reflect is the close correspondence between infants' developing knowledge of what human bodies look like, and what they do. We can not rule out this interpretation, but make two points against it: First, if the object exploration tasks reflected conceptual categorization based on what human bodies do, it is not clear why 15- and 18-month-olds should have shown differential sensitivity to the arms on head doll, but not have noticed the armless doll. A human body without arms is arguably more functionally disrupted than a human body with arms that happen to attach at the head. Second, in Study 7 we found that 12-month-olds' responses to a scrambled bowling pin were equivalent to their responses a scrambled doll in the object exploration paradigm. Since the bowling pin was designed to be a nonsense shape, it is not clear what would be the conceptual or functional basis for infants' responses to a change in the configuration of that object. Bowling pins do not do anything, so how could infants' responses to the scrambled version have been based on "what objects do" (Mandler, 2000, p. 3)?

Thus we conclude that in the current studies, the visual habituation and object exploration data reflected a single categorization process that distinguished scrambled from typical human body shapes, and the emergence of the capacity to make this categorical distinction reflected the development of detailed visuo-spatial human body knowledge in infancy.

GENERAL DISCUSSION

Several conclusions have been drawn and briefly discussed, based on the data presented in this monograph. First, there is a developmental dissociation between infants' responses to human faces and human bodies. Second, the pattern of results across the eight studies establishes a fairly clear developmental trajectory for the early development of visuo-spatial human body knowledge and further suggests that the earliest visuo-spatial representation of the human body is likely to be highly schematic. We now review and discuss these conclusions in detail, then turn to speculation about how the three different levels of human body knowledge—sensorimotor, visuo-spatial and lexical–semantic—may be related in development.

Faces and Bodies Are Processed Distinctly in Infancy

Our work has established different developmental trajectories for infants' responses to typical and scrambled face and bodies. As reviewed in Chapter I, visual preference studies established that the development of preferences for typical and scrambled faces and bodies developed independently (Slaughter et al., 2002). In the current series of studies, it was only between 15 and 18 months that infants discriminated scrambled from typical human bodies in visual and manual habituation paradigms. Compared to the well-documented face processing that has been demonstrated by infants early in the first year of life, the capacity to discriminate bodies develops surprisingly late. Whereas infants younger than 12 months can discriminate scrambled from typical faces, identify individuals based on their faces and discriminate faces on the basis of a number of abstract characteristics including gender, attractiveness, and emotional expression, in the current studies 12-month-olds showed no capacity for making the basic categorical discrimination between scrambled and typical bodies. These divergent developmental trajectories indicate that visuo-spatial knowledge of faces and bodies develop distinctly in infancy.

Recent neuroimaging studies similarly suggest a dissociation between aspects of face and body visual processing in the adult brain. When presented with pictures of faces versus pictures of bodies or body parts, distinct regions of the cortex are active, suggesting different underlying representations or processes are involved in the perception of faces and bodies. These studies arguably tap visuo-spatial representations because they require processing of static images reflecting structural and spatial attributes of faces and bodies (e.g., there is no motion, and no requirement for verbal responding). When presented with images of faces, adults typically demonstrate maximal activation in the ventral temporal lobe; this area has been dubbed the fusiform face area to reflect its consistent, selective activation during face perception (Kanwisher, et al., 1997). When presented with human body images, in contrast, a distinct region in the lateral occipitotemporal cortex, dubbed the extrastriate body area (Downing, Jiang, Shuman, & Kanwisher, 2001) is selectively active.[6] The extrastriate body area, or EBA, does not respond to human face stimuli, but is active when adults view pictures of full human bodies, as well as human body parts like hands and feet. It is responsive to schematic representations like stick figures and realistic images like color photographs. While it is admittedly a big leap from fMRI work with adults to behavior-based developmental studies, the dissociations of face and body processing in both strands of research are suggestive of distinct underlying representations for faces and bodies.

As noted in Chapter I however, there are also instances in which bodies and faces seem to be treated similarly by adults; for instance, some autotopagnosic patients tested have failed to successfully complete face puzzles as well as body puzzles (Guariglia, 2002; Ogden, 1985). In attempting both puzzles, patients made errors by substituting parts and/or mixing them up. If autotopagnosia is caused by brain damage that disrupts visuo-spatial body knowledge, then concurrent failure on face and body tasks suggests that the underlying representations for faces and bodies may be linked. Another example of similarity in responding to faces and bodies is Reed, Stone,

83

Bozova, and Tanaka's (2003) finding of a "body inversion effect" similar to the well-established face inversion effect, whereby adult participants took longer to identify body postures when they were presented upside down, in comparison to other inverted complex stimuli. Reed and colleagues concluded that bodies and faces are therefore subject to similar visual-processing constraints. Thus in adulthood, visual processing of bodies is similar to that of faces under some conditions.

When the patterns of similarities and differences in face and body processing are analyzed, it appears that tasks involving identification of a face or a body as such, lead to dissociations in performance for faces and bodies. Thus infants' categorization of bodies as typical or scrambled, and adults' perception of face and bodies in neuroimaging studies, point to distinct underlying representations for faces and bodies. In contrast, tasks involving more complex or higher-level processing, like matching tasks or construction tasks, may involve similar processing constraints for faces and bodies, such that the representations for faces and bodies are handled by the same cognitive machinery and therefore lead to similar task performance (Slaughter et al., in press).

In infancy, as the current studies have shown, there is a clear developmental dissociation in infants' responses to faces and bodies that may reflect at least partially independent underlying visuo-spatial representations. This finding can be explained in terms of several different, but complimentary, models that address different levels of explanation.

If we assume that visuo-spatial representations of faces and bodies are distinct, and both develop as a result of perceptual experience, faces may be learned about relatively early for purely perceptual reasons. Face patterns are arguably more internally consistent than body patterns, and they have high contrast that gets infants' attention. As infants are perceptually tuned to attend to high-contrast patterns (Banks & Dannemiller, 1987; Valenza et al., 1996), faces will pull more of their attention relative to bodies and therefore learning about faces will progress relatively quickly. Also, compared to faces, bodies are perceptually variable. Even in motion, the internal features of faces maintain their definitive configuration (e.g., two eyes on top, nose, and mouth below). Bodies on the other hand are far more plastic and even though the limbs remain connected to the torso at fixed points through body movements, the relative distances between limbs and the apparent shape of the limbs may vary widely. Thus it may take a relatively long time for infants to develop visuo-spatial representations that specify the typical structure of the human body simply because bodies, compared to faces, are perceptually less stable.

A second explanation for the dissociation infants' responses to face and bodies has to do with exposure: infants will have more experience of faces in the first year of life, as their mode of interaction in early infancy is most likely to be face-to-face (Stern, 1977; Trevarthan, 1979; Trevarthan & Hubley, 1978). Also infants' small stature and relatively poor upright postural control in the first half year of life may preclude them from getting much perceptual experience of full human bodies until they begin to sit up, or walk upright. Before that stage, infants' exposure to human bodies in the cannonical orientation and posture is likely to be limited. In fact, prewalkers may have a good deal of exposure to apparently scrambled bodies, as adults lean over and extend their arms to play with them, sit on the floor to interact with them, or bend down to pick them up. Although the current series of studies found no consistent evidence for a link between upright locomotion and the capacity to discriminate scrambled from typical body shapes, more careful postural and motor assessments might uncover such a link.

Third, at a social-evolutionary level, infants may be highly attuned to faces because they provide the most concentrated and useful information about other people; we identify individuals and interact with them in general, via their faces. If newborns are equipped with some innate template or perceptual bias that directs their attention to other humans (Bonatti, Frot, Zangl, & Mehler, 2002; Gopnik & Meltzoff, 1997; Johnson & Morton, 1991; Karmiloff-Smith, 1992), it seems likely that such innate predispositions would focus on the face as a quick route to identifying and engaging with other people. Along these lines, newborn chicks show a bias to preferentially attend to the face/head of conspecifics, while apparently ignoring the body. In filial preference/approach tests, where newborn chicks were dark-reared then exposed to static stimuli resembling adult fowl, chicks walked toward any stimulus that had the head of an adult fowl, even if the body underneath that head was scrambled, or even nonbiological (e.g., a box; Johnson & Horn, 1988). It may be that a similar inborn tendency exists in human infants, and they, like newborn chicks, are born with an innate perceptual bias that leads them to selectively attend to the head/face of conspecifics, while details of the body are ignored.

Any or all of these explanations may be relevant to the developmental dissociation in infants' responses to faces and bodies. Given the importance of faces in early social interactions, it may be appropriate to conceptualize that dissociation in terms of infants' having highly developed and precocious face processing skills, rather than viewing young infants as being slow to develop knowledge about the human body.

A different perspective is that visuo-spatial human body representations may develop not through perceptual experience, as suggested above, but through an alternate route. One such route (discussed in more detail in the next section) might be via redescription of earlier-developing sensori-motor body representations. If this were the case, then the dissociation in infants' face and body processing could simply reflect differential development of sensori-motor control over faces versus bodies. As motor development follows a cephalo-caudal pattern, sensori-motor representations of the face would presumably develop earlier than those of the rest of the body, and visuo-spatial representations, if derived from on sensori-motor ones, would also follow a face-first developmental pattern.

Developmental Trajectory for Visuo-spatial Human Body Knowledge

Based on the evidence presented in Chapters II and III, we propose that an initial visuo-spatial body representation emerges in the first year of life, and this representation is highly schematic, lacking in detail and inclusive enough to allow 12-month-olds to perceive scrambled human bodies as being acceptable versions of the human body category. This proposal agrees with Quinn and Eimas' (1998) hypothesis that the early categorization of humans is based on a broad, schematic representation that includes any animal with head/facial features and an elongated body. Similar to Quinn and Eimas, we propose that the early visuo-spatial body representation is defined by a head/face at the top of an elongated, vertically symmetrical body. Before 18 months of age or so, we suggest that infants are willing to accept any stimulus that conforms to this basic pattern, as being an acceptable human. This hypothesis explains the pattern of data that we have reported:

(a) Before 15–18 months of age, infants treated our scrambled human bodies as being categorically equivalent to typical human bodies. Thus before that age, infants' visuo-spatial body representation must be inclusive enough to include both our scrambled and typical human body shapes. In all the studies reported in Chapters II and III, both the scrambled and typical body stimuli conform to the hypothesized schematic template of a head at the top of an elongated symmetrical body.

(b) We found that 15- and 18-month-old infants in Study 6 were most sensitive to the arms on head doll. We propose that the arms on head scrambled body is the one that most obviously disrupts the hypothesized schematic body representation, by having the arms, however symmetrical, above the head/face. The piggy tail control doll presented in Study 8 to contrast with the arms on head doll did not disrupt this hypothesized schematic body representation, because on the basis of their color and texture, the raised piggy tails of that doll were not perceived as parts of the body that rightly belonged below the face/head.

(c) In Study 5, we found that 12-month-old infants made a categorical discrimination between scrambled and typical geobodies, even though infants of that age repeatedly failed to make the same discrimination for human bodies. This suggests that two different categorization processes were occurring in the two different conditions. As noted above, we suggest that infants passed the geobodies task because they had no pre-established

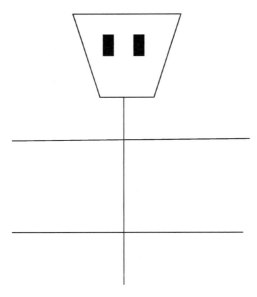

FIGURE 10.—Hypothesized schematic visuo-spatial body representation of infants under age 18 months: a head/face on top of an elongated, vertically symmetrical body.

representation for geobodies when they were presented in the experimental setup. Thus we propose that infants in Study 5 analyzed the abstract geobody shapes, generalized the typical pattern, and then noticed violations of that pattern in the test trials. When it came to human body shapes, on the other hand, we believe that infants came to the experiment with a pre-established representation, namely, a schematic, highly inclusive visuo-spatial body representation, that led them to classify all the bodies, including the scrambled ones, as being members of the same category. Thus young infants schematic visuo-spatial body representation precluded their making a categorical discrimination of scrambled versus typical human body shapes.

Figure 10 portrays the hypothesized schematic body representation of face/head on top and symmetry below. It is worth noting that this hypothesized body representation is perceptually similar to the human body drawings of toddlers and preschoolers aged two to four years (Cox, 1993). As our studies showed that by 2 years of age, discrimination of scrambled from typical bodies is fully developed, this implies that toddlers' knowledge of the visuo-spatial attributes of the human body is more sophisticated than their drawings reflect. As discussed in Chapter I, one explanation for this dissociation in toddler's body drawings and their visuo-spatial body knowledge is that young children's drawings are constrained by their perceptual-motor abilities such that they do not put to paper everything they know about the human body shape. However, another possibility is that the hypothesized schematic visuo-spatial body representation may remain intact, underpinning the development of a more detailed representation and supporting reasoning and behaviour in some situations. These might include situations that are cognitively and motorically taxing, such as drawing, or alternatively, any situation in which toddlers must access their visuo-spatial body knowledge at a symbolic level (e.g., drawing, body part naming/localization). If so, it may be possible to find other situations in which older children, and even adults, fall back on the initial, schematic, head on top/symmetry below body representation. Relevant examples again can be found in clinical neuropsychological case studies: When Guariglia et al.'s (2002) autotopagnosic patient was asked to put together human body puzzles, his patterns were inaccurate but did include a head on top and a symmetrically organized body (in which the two halves of the torso were separated by a wide gap and the legs were right–left reversed). Similarly, Ogden's (1985) autotopagnosic patient drew a human stick figure with a face on top of a symmetrical torso with arms and legs, but placed hands and feet in incorrect positions when prompted to draw more detail (e.g., the feet were put on the ends of the arms). Thus the human/animal categorization studies (Quinn & Eimas, 1998), our scrambled versus typical discrimination studies, toddlers' human figure drawings and some aspects of autotopagnosic patients' performance all support the hypothesis that the initial, most basic visuo-spatial human body representation is highly schematic and characterized by a head on top of a vertically symmetrical body.

Now we turn to the question how this schematic visuo-spatial body representation originates. We envision three possibilities. The first is that the schematic visuo-spatial body representation is innate, as is sometimes proposed for schematic face representations. The second possibility is that visuo-spatial body knowledge develops directly from infants' perceptual experiences with their own and others' bodies. A third possibility is that visuo-spatial body knowledge derives from earlier-developing sensori-motor body knowledge, as a result of some sort of developmental process. We now discuss these possibilities in turn.

As reviewed in Chapter I, one model proposed to explain newborns' preferences for human face stimuli is that these stimuli conform to an innate, schematic human face template (Johnson & Morton, 1991). If true, then it is possible that this proposed innate face representation actually continues below the chin and includes the whole schematic body pattern portrayed in Figure 10. This is one hypothesis for the origin of visuo-spatial human body knowledge. Since previous studies with newborns have not assessed responses to human body images other than disembodied faces, we simply may not know the full extent of newborns' knowledge of the structure of the human body. On this view, the hypothesized face template investigated in previous research would be only a part of the innate representation available to young infants, namely, the top of a complete visuo-spatial body representation that would also include an elongated symmetrical body below the face. Given that faces and bodies are almost always attached to each other in the natural environment, this may be a reasonable proposal. In order to test it, we would have to carry out studies that test very young infants' capacity to recognize violations of the hypothesized schematic body representation, perhaps by placing the head at the bottom of the pattern, or making the body asymmetrical. As noted above, we have observed that moving the head from the top of a human body image seriously disrupts adults' recognition of the pattern as a human body; perhaps newborns would show a similar sensitivity to patterns that violate the schematic human body pattern. If so, that would suggest that the initial, schematic visuo-spatial human body representation is present at birth.

A second hypothesis for the origin of visuo-spatial body knowledge is that it develops directly from perceptual experience of our own and other people's bodies. We already outlined above how faces and bodies may be subject to different experiential constraints that could account for the developmental dissociation in the emergence of detailed visuo-spatial representations for each. In terms of a developmental process, visual experience of one's own and other people's bodies (as well as representations portraying human bodies) might be subject to perceptual analysis, perhaps like that described by Mandler (1988, 1992, 2000), that would give rise to the schematic visuo-spatial body representation first, then fill in the perceptual details within the first 15–18 months of life. According to Mandler, infants have an innate capacity to perceptually analyze the visual world, and the perceptual system extracts schematic representations that structure further perception and learning in a given domain. Although Mandler's schematic representations ("image schemas") are typically highly abstract and movement based, this model has the advantage, from our perspective, of being consistent with the schematic-to-detailed developmental trajectory for visuo-spatial body knowledge that we have hypothesized.

A final option, mentioned briefly above, is that visuo-spatial and lexical–semantic human body knowledge derive from earlier-developing sensori-motor body representations. As reviewed in Chapter I, it appears that sensori-motor body representations may emerge in the first year of life and detailed visuo-spatial body knowledge, as we have demonstrated, emerges in the second year. The first elements of the lexical–semantic level of body knowledge are also acquired in the toddler period. If these levels of human body knowledge are related, then the following developmental trajectory may be implicated: sensori-motor body representations participate in the development of visuo-spatial and lexical–semantic body knowledge. As noted in Chapter I, this has been a popular hypothesis in the neuropsychological literature (Buxbaum & Coslett, 2001; Poeck & Orgass,

1971; Sirigu et al., 1991) based on the proximity of brain regions where these levels of body knowledge are thought to be instantiated, and in the developmental literature (Piaget, 1953) based on classic models of cognitive development. This developmental hypothesis is also consistent with more recent models of cognitive development that also assume early sensori-motor knowledge is the basis for later representational knowledge. For instance, according to Karmiloff-Smith's (1992) theory of representational redescription (RR), all cognitive representations originate as implicit, procedural sensori-motor schemes, and development involves an iterative, four-stage process of representational redescription, whereby representations become progressively more accessible to consciousness, more explicit and more manipulable. On this view, sensori-motor body knowledge, instantiated in built-in motor, postural and intermodal neural circuitry, would be the foundation for the other two levels of human body knowledge, but would also function as productive cognitive structures at the implicit, procedural level throughout life. According to the RR model, sensori-motor human body knowledge, represented at Karmiloff-Smith's nonconscious, automatic, procedural Level 1, would be endogenously redescribed to generate representations at the more abstract, flexible but still nonconscious E1 level, sometime in the first year of life. This E1-level representation might be the schematic visuo-spatial body representation that we propose as being a head/face on top, symmetry below template. Then around 18 months, this E1-level representation would be redescribed again, giving rise to a potentially conscious, detailed representation that supports discrimination of scrambled and typical human body shapes (at Karmiloff-Smith's E2 level). This model accommodates our data, and further, could explain the hierarchical acquisition of lexical–semantic body knowledge: Early on, toddlers may learn words for those parts of the visuo-spatial representation that are represented at the E1 level, namely, parts of the head and face and the limbs. Toddlers' lexical–semantic knowledge may then be elaborated alongside the redescriptive development of the more detailed visuo-spatial representation starting around 15–18 months of age.

In relation to this model, it is worth noting that in some autotopagnosic patients, the lesions that produce localizing autotopagnosia are dorsal as opposed to ventral, meaning that they are evident in the "where" processing stream that is typically associated with perception and interpretation of dynamic stimuli, rather than in the "what" stream typically associated with featural processing (Buxbaum & Coslett, 2001). This tentatively supports the idea that (featural) visuo-spatial body representations may derive from anatomically nearby (dynamic) sensori-motor representations.

The RR model nicely outlines how visuo-spatial and lexical–semantic levels of body representation may derive from sensori-motor body knowledge. Unfortunately, one feature of the RR model does not agree with the developmental data we have presented: Within the RR model, redescriptions are thought to result in representations that are progressively more abstract and less detailed. As outlined above, we propose that visuo-spatial body representations originate in a highly schematic form, becoming, in contrast, more detailed with development by the middle of the second year of life. Thus we propose an abstract-to-specific developmental trajectory for visuo-spatial human body knowledge (Bower, 1989; Bower & Wishart, 1979), whereby infants' initial visuo-spatial body knowledge contains the essential, core elements of human body structure (e.g., head on top; symmetrical body below), and that representation becomes more detailed and complete over time. This does not preclude the possibility that visuo-spatial body knowledge derives from sensori-motor body knowledge, but suggests that further work is necessary to establish how later-developing visuo-spatial body knowledge might be related to earlier-developing representations of the structure of the human body.

The RR model explicitly states that as development progresses, different levels of representation in a given domain continue to exist, and each level supports cognitive functioning that relies on representations at the given level of description. Similarly, if the schematic visuo-spatial human body representation is innately specified, or represented as an image schema derived from perceptual experience, then on those models as well, the schematic body representation would remain intact even as more detailed visuo-spatial body knowledge was acquired. In this context it is interesting to note the general configural qualities of "impossible" human figure drawings that were generated by children in Karmiloff-Smith's (1990) study. When asked to draw "a person that doesn't exist," children between the ages of five and 11 altered the basic human body shape in several ways: they added elements (extra limbs, a second head), deleted elements (left out an eye or a leg), inserted elements from other object categories, and the like. Figure 11 portrays an example of a spontaneously drawn impossible human ("a monster" in the 5-year-old artists' words) that is similar to the prompted examples generated by Karmiloff-Smith's (1990) participants. The important point is that these creative representations of impossible humans are striking in that they almost invariably portray a head on top of an elongated, symmetrical body. Thus it seems possible that when asked to generate representations of impossible humans, for which no detailed knowledge already exists, children (and some adults) may fall back on the earliest, schematic representation of the visuo-spatial features of the human body. This argument has already been offered to explain the prominence of tadpole drawings in 2- to 3-year-olds; when faced with the task of drawing a human figure, the demands of the task might force toddlers to rely on their most basic knowledge of human body structure; the early-developing, schematic visuo-spatial representation of a head on top of an elongated,

FIGURE 11.—Spontaneous drawing of an impossible human, produced by a 5-year-old girl. Note the adherence to the hypothesized schematic body representation defined as head on top and symmetrical body below.

symmetrical body. Similarly, the spare, child-like stick figure drawing of Ogden's (1985) autotopagnosic patient could also have been generated with reference to the early developing schematic body representation that may have remained intact despite damage to later-developing, more elaborate visuo-spatial body representations.

We have offered three developmental hypotheses that could accommodate the data presented in Chapters II and III. Further work is required to test these competing models. As discussed above, studies that present newborns with a variety of both face and body patterns could shed light on whether an innate body template exists. While we found no consistent evidence for a link between motor development and visuo-spatial body knowledge in the current studies, additional studies that include more careful sensori-motor assessments might clarify the relative importance of perceptual and motor experience to the early development of visuo-spatial human body knowledge.

Origins and Early Development of Human Body Knowledge

In Chapter I we reviewed literature on infants' and toddlers' human body knowledge in terms of the three-level framework derived from cognitive neuropsychological research. That framework indicates that in the adult brain, human body knowledge is specialized such that sensori-motor, visuo-spatial and lexical–semantic body knowledge are instantiated in distinct, partially independent levels of representation. As discussed in the introductory chapter, these specialized levels of body knowledge can be further analyzed in terms of developmental levels of representation, leading to a more complete developmental picture. We conclude with speculation about this complete developmental picture. Sensori-motor body knowledge progressively encompasses congenital bodily coordinations (e.g., reflexes), motor/postural control, and sensori-motor body representations that may be implicated in facial imitation, self-other discrimination and perception of PLDs. The visuo-spatial level of body knowledge also encompasses different developmental levels: animal-human discrimination tasks implicate the presence of a schematic visuo-spatial body representation available in the first 6 months of life, and, as we have argued, that representation develops in detail over the next year, allowing infants to recognize categorical distinctions among human body types in our typical scrambled discrimination tasks. Somewhat later in development, toddlers begin to access their visuo-spatial body knowledge at a symbolic level, when they begin to identify body parts and draw human bodies. Around the same time, lexical–semantic body knowledge begins to emerge; this level of body knowledge is necessarily symbolic, as these representations are based in language. Thus within the first few years of life, toddlers acquire human body knowledge at a number of different levels of representation, and at progressively greater levels of complexity. This monograph has explored the development of visuo-spatial body knowledge in detail. Further work is required to understand how levels of body knowledge interact in typical development, giving rise to the rich, complex and coherent knowledge about the human body that is characteristic of adult cognition.

NOTE

6. Note that this location is distinct from the parietal locations that are typically associated with autotopagnosia and other "disorders of the body schema." This discrepancy has not been addressed in the published literature, though it is often acknowledged that human body knowledge is likely to be widely distributed in the brain (Graziano & Botvinick, 2002).

REFERENCES

Abranvel, E., & Sigafoos, A. (1984). Exploring the presence of imitation during early infancy. *Child Development*, **55**, 381–392.

Adolph, K. (1997). Learning in the development of infant locomotion. *Monographs of the Society for Research in Child Development*, **56** (3, Serial No. 251).

Adolph, K. (2000). Specificity of learning: Why infants fall over a veritable cliff. *Psychological Science*, **11**, 290–295.

Andersen, E. (1978). Lexical universals of body-part terminolgy. In H. Greenberg (Ed.), *Universals in human language* (Vol. 3, pp. 335–368). Stanford, CA: Stanford University Press.

Anisfeld, M. (1991). Neonatal imitation: Review. *Developmental Review*, **11**, 60–97.

Anisfeld, M. (1996). Only tongue protrusion modelling is matched by neonates. *Developmental Review*, **16**, 149–161.

Bahrick, L., & Watson, J. S. (1985). Detection of intermodal proprioceptive-visual contingency as a potential basis of self-perception in infancy. *Developmental Psychology*, **21**, 963–973.

Banks, M., & Dannemiller, J. (1987). Infant visual psychophysics. In P. Salapatek & L. Cohen (Eds.), *Handbook of infant perception, Vol. 1, from sensation to perception* (pp. 115–184). Orlando, FL: Academic Press.

Bayley, N. (1969). *Bayley scales of infant development*. New York: Psychological Corporation.

Bertenthal, B. (1993). Infants' perception of biomechanical motions: intrinsic image and knowledge-based constraints. In C. E. Granrud (Ed.), *Visual perception and cognition in infancy* (pp. 175–214). Hillsdale, NJ: Lawrence Erlbaum Associates.

Bertenthal, B., Haith, M., & Campos, J. (1983). The partial lag design: A method for controlling spontaneous regression in the infant-control habituation paradigm. *Infant Behavior and Development*, **6**, 331–338.

Bertenthal, B., Proffitt, D., & Cutting, J. (1984). Infant sensitivity to figural coherence in biomechanical motions. *Journal of Experimental Child Psychology*, **37**, 213–230.

Bertenthal, B., Proffitt, D., Kramer, S., & Spetner, N. (1987). Infants' encoding of kinetic displays varying in relative coherence. *Developmental Psychology*, **23** (2), 171–178.

Bonatti, L., Frot, E., Zangl, R., & Mehler, J. (2002). The human first hypothesis: Identification of conspecifics and individuation of objects in the young infant. *Cognitive Psychology*, **44** (4), 388–426.

Bornstein, M., & Krinsky, S. (1985). Perception of symmetry in infancy: The salience of vertical symmetry and the perception of pattern wholes. *Journal of Experimental Child Psychology*, **41**, 49–60.

Bower, T. (1989). *The rational infant*. New York: W. H. Freeman & Company.

Bower, T., & Wishart, G. (1979). Towards a unitary theory of development. In E. Thoman (Ed.), *Origins of the infant's social responsiveness* (pp. 66–93). Hillsdale, NJ: Lawrence Erlbaum Associates.

Brazelton, T., Nugent, J., & Lester, B. (1987). Neonatal behavioural assessment scale. In J. Osofsky (Ed.), *Handbook of infant development* (2nd ed., pp. 780–817). New York: Wiley.

Bremner, J. (2000). Developmental relationships between perception and action in infancy. *Infant Behaviour and Development*, **23**, 567–582.

Brittain, W., & Chien, Y. (1983). Relationship between preschool children's ability to name body parts and their ability to construct a man. *Perceptual and Motor Skills*, **57**, 19–24.

Butterworth, G., & Hopkins, B. (1988). Hand-mouth coordination in the newborn human infant. *British Journal of development Psychology*, **6**, 303–314.

Buxbaum, L., & Coslett, H. (2001). Specialized structural descriptions for human body parts: Evidence from autotopagnosia. *Cognitive Neuropsychology*, **18**, 289–306.

Carey, D. (1996). Neurophysiology: "Monkey see, monkey do" cells. *Current Biology*, **6**, 1087–1088.

Coslett, H. (1988). Evidence for a disturbance of the body schema in neglect. *Brain and Cognition*, **37**, 527–544.

Coslett, H., Sattran, E., & Schwoebel, J. (2002). Knowledge of the human body: A distinct schematic domain. *Neurology*, **59**, 357–363.

Cox, M. (1993). *Children's drawings of the human figure*. Hove: Erlbaum.

Cox, M., & Lambon, R. (1996). Young children's ability to adapt their drawings of the human figure. *Educational Psychology*, **16**, 245–255.

Crowe, S., & Prescott, T. (2003). Continuity and change in the development of category structure: Insights from the semantic fluency task. *International Journal of Behavioural Development*, **27**, 467–479.

DeLoache, J. (1995). Early symbol understanding and use. In D. Medin (Ed.), *The psychology of learning and motivation* (pp. 65–114). New York: Academic Press.

DeLoache, J. (2000). Dual representation and young children's use of scale models. *Child Development*, **71**, 329–338.

DeLoache, J., & Marzolf, D. (1995). The use of dolls to interview young children: Issues of symbolic representation. *Journal of Experimental Child Psychology*, **60**, 155–173.

DeLoache, J., Pierroutsakos, S., & Uttal, D. (2003). The origins of pictorial competence. *Current Directions in Psychological Science*, **12**, 114–118.

DeLoache, J., & Smith, C. (1999). Early symbolic representation. In I. Sigel (Ed.), *Development of mental representation: Theories and applications*. Mahwah, NJ: Lawrence Erlbaum Associates.

Denes, G. (1989). Disorders of body awareness and body knowledge. In F. Boller & J. Grafman (Eds.), *Handbook of neuropsychology* (Vol. 2, pp. 207–228). Amsterdam: Elsevier Science Publishers.

Denes, G., Cappelletti, J., Zilli, T., Dalla Porta, F., & Gallana, A. (2000). A category-specific deficit of spatial representation: The case of autotopagnosia. *Neuropsychologia*, **38**, 345–350.

Dennis, M. (1976). Dissociated naming and location of body parts after left anterior temporal lobe resection: An experimental case study. *Brain and Language*, **3**, 147–163.

DeRenzi, E., & Scotti, G. (1970). Autotopagnosia: Fiction or reality? Report of a case. *Archives of Neurology*, **23**, 221–227.

Downing, P., Jiang, Y., Shuman, M., & Kanwisher, N. (2001). A cortical area selective for visual processing of the human body. *Science*, **293**, 23–26.

Elian, N., Marcel, A., & Bermudez, J. (1995). Self-consciousness and the body: An interdisciplinary introduction. In J. Bermúdez, A. Marcel & N. Eilan (Eds.), *The body and the self* (pp. 1–28). Cambridge: MIT/Bradford Press.

Fantz, R. L. (1963). Pattern vision in newborn infants. *Science*, **140**, 296–297.

Felician, O., Ceccaldi, M., Didic, M., Thinus-Blanc, C., & Poncet, M. (2003). Pointing to body parts: A double dissociation study. *Neuropsychologia*, **41**, 1307–1316.

Field, T., Cohen, D., Garcia, R., & Greenberg, R. (1984). Mother-stranger face discrimination by the newborn. *Infant Behavior and Development*, **7**, 19–27.

Field, T., Woodson, T., Greenberg, T., & Cohen, D. (1982). Discrimination and imitation of facial expressions by neonates. *Science*, **218**, 178–181.

Fox, R., & McDaniel, C. (1982). The perception of biological motion by human infants. *Science*, **218**, 486–487.

Freeman, N. (1987). Current problems in the development of representational picture-production. *Archives de Psychologie*, **55**, 127–152.

Gallagher, S. (1995). Body schema and intentionality. In J. Bermúdez, A. Marcel & N. Eilan (Eds.), *The body and the self* (pp. 225–244). Cambridge: MIT/Bradford Press.

Gallagher, S. (2004). *Before you know it: How the body shapes the mind*. Oxford, UK: Oxford University Press.

Gallagher, S., Butterworth, G., Lew, A., & Cole, J. (1998). Hand–mouth coordination, congenital absence of limb, and evidence for innate body schemas. *Brain and Cognition*, **38**, 53–65.

Gallagher, S., & Meltzoff, A. (1996). The earliest sense of self and others: Merleau-Ponty and recent developmental studies. *Philosophical Psychology*, **9**, 213–236.

Gallese, V., Fadiga, L., Fogassi, L., & Rizzolatti, G. (1996). Action recognition in the premotor cortex. *Brain*, **119** (Part 2), 593–609.

Gallese, V., Fadiga, L., Fogassi, L., & Rizzolatti, G. (2002). Action representation and the inferior parietal lobule. In W. Prinz & B. Hommel (Eds.), *Common mechanisms in perception and action: Attention and performance XIX* (pp. 381–400). Oxford: Oxford University Press.

Gellert, E. (1962). Children's conceptions of the content and functions of the human body. *Genetic Psychology Monographs*, **65**, 293–405.

Gesell, A. (1940). *The first five years of life*. New York: Harper & Row.

Goldenberg, G. (1997). Disorders of body perception. In T. Feinberg & M. Farah (Eds.), *Behavioral neurology and neuropsychology* (pp. 289–297). New York: McGraw-Hill.

Gopnik, A., & Meltzoff, A. (1997). *Words, thoughts, and theories*. Cambridge, MA: MIT Press.

Goren, C., Sarty, M., & Wu, P. (1975). Visual following and pattern discrimination of face-like stimuli by newborn infants. *Pediatrics*, **56**, 544–549.

Graziano, M., & Botvinick, M. (2002). How the brain represents the body: Insights from neurophysiology and psychology. In W. Prinz & B. Hommel (Eds.), *Common mechanisms in perception and action: Attention and performance XIX* (pp. 136–157). Oxford: Oxford University Press.

Guajardo, J., & Woodward, A. (2002). Infants attend to surface features in identifying goal-directed agents. Paper presented at the International Conference on Infant Studies, Toronto, Canada, April.

Guariglia, C., Piccardi, L., Puglisi Allegra, M., & Traballesi, M. (2002). Is autotopagnosia real? EC says yes. A case study. *Neuropsychologia*, **40**, 1744–1749.

Haith, M. (1998). Who put the cog in infant cognition? Is rich interpretation too costly? *Infant Behavior and Development*, **21**, 167–179.

Haith, M., & Benson, J (1998). Infant cognition. In W. Damon, D. Kuhn & R. Siegler (Eds.), *Handbook of child psychology: Cognition, perception and language* (5th ed., pp. 199–254). New York: John Wiley & Sons.

Harris, D. (1963). *Children's drawings as measures of intellectual maturity: A revision and extension of the Goodenough Draw-a-Man Test*. New York: Harcourt, Brace and World.

von Hofsten, C. (1982). Eye-hand coordination in the newborn. *Developmental Psychology*, **18**, 450–461.

Hunter, M., Ames, E., & Koopman, R. (1983). Effects of stimulus complexity and familiarization time on infant preferences for novel and familiar stimuli. *Developmental Psychology*, **19**, 338–352.

Inagaki, K., & Hatano, G. (2002). *Young children's naïve thinking about the biological world*. New York: Psychology Press.

Jaakkola, K., & Slaughter, V. (2002). Children's body knowledge: Understanding "life" as a biological goal. *British Journal of Developmental Psychology*, **20**, 325–342.

Jacobson, S. (1979). Matching behaviour in the young infant. *Child Development*, **50**, 425–430.

Johansson, G. (1973). Visual perception of biological motion and a model for its analysis. *Perception and Psychophysics*, **14**, 201–211.

Johnson, C., & Kendrick, K. (1984). Body partonomy: How children partition the human body. *Developmental Psychology*, **20**, 967–974.

Johnson, L., Perlmutter, M., & Trabasso, T. (1979). The leg bone is connected to the knee bone: Children's representation of body parts in memory, drawing and language. *Child Development*, **59**, 1192–1202.

Johnson, M. (1987). *The body in the mind*. Chicago: University of Chicago Press.

Johnson, M. H. (1997). *Developmental cognitive neuroscience*. Cambridge, MA: Blackwell.

Johnson, M. H., Dziurawiec, S., Ellis, H., & Morton, J. (1991). Newborns' preferential tracking of face-like stimuli and its subsequent decline. *Cognition*, **40**, 1–19.

Johnson, M. H., & Horn, G. (1988). Development of filial preferences in dark-reared chicks. *Animal Behavior*, **36**, 675–683.

Johnson, M. H., & Morton, J. (1991). *Biology and cognitive development: The case of face recognition*. Oxford: Basil Blackwell Ltd.

Jones, S. (1996). Imitation or exploration: Young infants' matching of adults' oral gestures. *Child Development*, **67**, 1952–1969.

Kanwisher, N., McDermott, J., & Chun, M. (1997). The fusiform face area: A module in human extrastriate cortex specialized for face perception. *The Journal of Neuroscience*, **17**, 4302–4311.

Karmiloff-Smith, A. (1990). Constraints on representational change: Evidence from children's drawing. *Cognition*, **34**, 57–83.

Karmiloff-Smith, A. (1992). *Beyond modularity: A developmental perspective on cognitive science*. Cambridge, MA: MIT Press.

Lakoff, G. (1987). *Women, fire, and dangerous things: What categories reveal about the mind*. Chicago: University of Chicago Press.

Langer, J., Gillette, P., & Arriaga, R. (2003). Toddlers' cognition of adding and subtracting objects in action and in perception. *Cognitive Development*, **18**, 233–246.

Langlois, J., Roggman, L., Casey, R., Ritter, J., Rieser-Danner, L., & Jenkins, V. (1987). Infant preferences for attractive faces: Rudiments of a stereotype? *Developmental Psychology*, **23** (3), 363–369.

Lefford, A., Birch, H., & Green, G. (1974). The perceptual and cognitive bases for finger localization and selective finger movement in preschool children. *Child Development*, **45**, 335–343.

Legerstee, M. (1991). The role of person and object in eliciting early imitation. *Journal of Experimental Child Psychology*, **5**, 423–433.

MacWhinney, K., Cermak, S., & Fisher, A. (1987). Body part identification in 1- to 4-year-old children. *The American Journal of Occupational Therapy*, **41** (7), 454–459.

Mandler, J. (1988). How to build a baby: On the development of an accessible representational system. *Cognitive Development*, **3**, 113–136.

Mandler, J. (1992). How to build a baby II: Conceptual primitives. *Psychological Review*, **99**, 587–604.

Mandler, J. (1997). Development of categorization: Perceptual and conceptual categories. In G. Bremner, A. Slater & G. Butterworth (Eds.), *Infant development: Recent advances* (pp. 165–189). Hove, England: Psychology Press.

Mandler, J. (1998). Representation. In D. Kuhn & R. Siegler (Eds.), *Handbook of child psychology. Vol. 2, cognition, perception, and language* (W. Damon (Series Ed.) (pp. 255–308)). New York: Wiley.

Mandler, J. (2000). Perceptual and conceptual processes in infancy. *Journal of Cognition and Development*, **1**, 3–36.

Mandler, J., & McDonough, L. (1993). Concept formation in infancy. *Cognitive Development*, **8**, 291–318.

Mandler, J., & McDonough, L. (1996). Drinking and driving don't mix: Inductive generalization in infancy. *Cognition*, **59**, 307–335.

Mandler, J., & McDonough, L. (1998). On developing a knowledge base in infancy. *Developmental Psychology*, **34** (6), 1274–1288.

Mareschal, D., & Quinn, P. (2001). Categorization in infancy. *Trends in Cognitive Sciences*, **5** (10), 443–449.

Martineau, J., & Cochin, S. (2003). Visual perception in children: Human, animal and virtual movement activates different cortical areas. *International Journal of Psychophysiology*, **51**, 37–44.

Maurer, D. (1985). Infants' perception of facedness. In T. Field & N. Fox (Eds.), *Social perception in infants* (pp. 73–100). Norwood, NJ: Ablex Publishing.

McCarthy, G., Puce, A., Gore, J., & Allison, T. (1997). Face-specific processing in the human fusiform gyrus. *Journal of Cognitive Neuroscience*, **9**, 605–610.

Meltzoff, A., & Borton, R. (1979). Intermodal matching by human neonates. *Nature*, **282**, 403–404.

Meltzoff, A., & Gopnik, A. (1993). The role of imitation in understanding persons and developing a theory of mind. In S. Baron-Cohen, J. Tager-Flusberg & D. Cohen (Eds.), *Understanding other minds: Perspectives from autism* (pp. 335–366). New York: Oxford University Press.

Meltzoff, A., Kuhl, P., & Moore, K. (1991). Perception, representation, and the control of action in newborns and young infants: Toward a new synthesis. In M. Weiss & P. Zelazo (Eds.), *Newborn attention: Biological constraints and the influence of experience* (pp. 377–411). Westport, CT: Ablex Publishing.

Meltzoff, A., & Moore, K. (1977). Imitation of facial and manual gestures by human neonates. *Science*, **198**, 75–78.

Meltzoff, A., & Moore, K. (1983). Newborn infants imitate adult facial gestures. *Child Development*, **54**, 702–709.

Meltzoff, A., & Moore, K. (1989). Imitation in newborn infants: Exploring the range of gestures imitated and the underlying mechanisms. *Developmental Psychology*, **25**, 954–962.

Meltzoff, A., & Moore, K. (1995). Infants' understanding of people and things: From body imitation to folk psychology. In J. Bermúdez, A. Marcel & N. Eilan (Eds.), *The body and the self*. Cambridge: MIT/Bradford Press.

Meltzoff, A., & Moore, K. (1997). Explaining facial imitation: A theoretical model. *Early Development and Parenting*, **6**, 179–192.

Moore, D., Hobson, R., & Anderson, M. (1995). Person perception—does it involve IQ-independent perceptual processing? *Intelligence*, **20**, 65–86.

Moore, D., Hobson, R., & Lee, A. (1997). Components of person-perception: An investigation with autistic non-autistic retarded and typically developing children and adolescents. *British Journal of Developmental Psychology*, **15**, 401–423.

Morgan, R., & Rochat, P. (1997). Intermodal calibration of the body in early infancy. *Ecological Psychology*, **9**, 1–23.

Müller, U., & Overton, W. (1998). How to grow a baby: A reevaluation of image-schema and Piagetian action approaches to representation. *Human Development*, **41**, 71–111.

Müller, U., Sokol, B., & Overton, W. (1998). Reframing a constructivist model of the development of mental representations: The role of higher-order operations. *Developmental Review*, **18**, 155–201.

Nelson, C. (1987). The recognition of facial expressions in the first two years of life: Mechanisms of development. *Child Development*, **58**, 1157–1167.

Neisser, U. (1988). Five kinds of self-knoweldge. *Philsophical Psychology*, **1**, 35–59.

Oakes, L., Madole, K., & Cohen, L. (1991). Infants' object examining: Habituation and categorization. *Cognitive Development*, **6**, 377–392.

Oakes, L., Plumert, J., Lansink, J., & Merryman, J. (1996). Evidence for task-dependent categorization in infancy. *Infant Behavior and Development*, **19**, 425–440.

Ogden, J. (1985). Autotopagnosia: Occurrence in a patient without nominal aphasia and with an intact ability to point to parts of animals and objects. *Brain*, **108**, 1009–1022.

Overton, W. (1994). The arrow of time and the cycle of time: Concepts of change, cognition, and embodiment. *Psychological Inquiry*, **5**, 215–237.

Pauen, S. (2000). Early differentiation within the animate domain: Are humans something special? *Journal of Experimental Child Psychology*, **75**, 134–151.

Perner, J. (1991). *Understanding the representational mind*. Cambridge, MA: Bradford Books.

Piaget, J. (1953). *The origin of intelligence in the child*. London: Routledge & Kegan Paul Ltd.

Piaget, J. (1962). *Play, dreams and imitation in childhood*. New York: W.W. Norton & Co.

Poeck, K., & Orgass, B. (1971). The concept of the body schema: A critical review and some experimental results. *Cortex*, **7** (3), 254–277.

Quinn, P. (2002). Is the asymmetry in young infants' categorization of humans versus nonhuman animals based on head, body, or global gestalt information? Paper presented at the International Conference on Infant Studies, Toronto, Canada, April.

Quinn, P., & Eimas, P. (1996). Perceptual cues that permit categorical differentiation of animal species by infants. *Journal of Experimental Child Psychology*, **63**, 189–211.

Quinn, P., & Eimas, P. (1998). Evidence for global categorical representation of humans by young infants. *Journal of Experimental Child Psychology*, **69**, 151–174.

Quinn, P., & Eimas, P. (2000). The emergence of category representations during infancy: Are separate perceptual and conceptual processes required? *Journal of Cognition and Development*, **1**, 55–61.

Quinn, P., Johnson, M., Mareschal, D., Rakison, D., & Younger, B. (2000). Understanding early categorization: One process or two? *Infancy*, **1**, 111–122.

Reed, C. (2002). What is the body schema? In A. Meltzoff & W. Prinz (Eds.), *The imitative mind* (pp. 233–246). Cambridge: Cambridge University Press.

Reed, C., & Farah, M. (1995). The psychological reality of the body schema: A test with normal participants. *Journal of Experimental Psychology: Human Perception and Performance*, **21**, 334–343.

Reed, C., Stone, V., Bozova, S., & Tanaka, J. (2003). The body inversion effect. *Psychological Science*, **14**, 302–308.

Rochat, P. (Ed.) (1995). *The self in infancy: Theory and research*. Elsevier: Amsterdam.

Rochat, P. (1998). Self perception and action in infancy. *Experimental Brain Research*, **123**, 102–109.

Rochat, P., & Morgan, R. (1995). Spatial determinants in the perception of self-produced leg movements in 3- to 5-month-old infants. *Developmental Psychology*, **31**, 626–636.

Ronnqvist, L., & von Hofsten, C. (1994). Neonatal finger and arm movements as determined by a social and an object context. *Early Development and Parenting*, **3**, 81–94.

Ross, G. (1980). Categorization in 1- to 2-year-olds. *Developmental Psychology*, **16** (5), 391–396.

Schmuckler, M. A. (1996). Visual–proprioceptive intermodal perception in infancy. *Infant Behavior and Development*, **19**, 221–232.

Schmuckler, M., & Fairhall, J. (2001). Visual–proprioceptive intermodal perception using point light displays. *Child Development, 72*, 949–962.

Semenza, C. (1988). Impairment in localization of body parts following brain damage. *Cortex, 24*, 443–449.

Shiffrar, M. (2001). The visual interpretation of object and human movement. In T. Shipley & P. Kellman (Eds.), *From fragments to objects—segmentation and grouping in vision* (pp. 483–508). Amsterdam: Elsevier Science.

Shiffrar, M., & Pinto, J. (2002). The visual analysis of bodily motion. In W. Prinz & B. Hommel (Eds.), *Common mechanisms in perception and action: Attention and performance XIX* (pp. 381–400). Oxford: Oxford University Press.

Siegal, M., & Peterson, C. (1999). *Children's understanding of biology and health.* Cambridge: Cambridge University Press. (Cambridge Studies in Cognitive and Perceptual Development).

Simon, T. (1997). Reconceptualizing the origins of number knowledge: A "non-numerical" account. *Cognitive Development, 12*, 349–372.

Sirigu, A., Grafman, J., Bressler, K., & Sunderland, T. (1991). Multiple representations contribute to body knowledge processing. *Brain, 114*, 629–642.

Slater, A., Von der Schulenburg, C., Brown, E., Badenoch, M., Butterworth, G., Parsons, S., & Samuels, C. (1998). Newborn infants prefer attractive faces. *Infant Behaviour and Development, 21* (2), 345–354.

Slaughter, V., Heron, M., & Sim, S. (2002). Development of preferences for the human body shape in infancy. *Cognition, 85* (3), B71–B81.

Slaughter, V., Stone, V., & Reed, C. (in press). Perception of faces and bodies: Similar or different? *Current Directions in Psychological Science.*

Stern, D. (1977). *The first relationship: Infant and mother.* Glasgow: Fontana/Open Books.

Stern, D. (1985). *The interpersonal world of the infant.* New York: Basic Books.

Suddendorf, T. (2003). Early representational insight: 24-month-olds can use a photo to find an object in the world. *Child Development, 74*, 896–904.

Suddendorf, T., & Whiten, A. (2001). Mental evolution and development: Evidence for secondary representation in children, great apes and other animals. *Psychological Bulletin, 74*, 629–650.

Tanaka, J., & Gauthier, I. (1997). Expertise in object and face recognition. In R. Goldstone, P. Schyns & D. Medin (Eds.), *Psychology of learning and motivation, Vol. 36: Perceptual mechanisms of learning* (pp. 83–125). San Diego, CA: Academic Press.

Thelen, E. (1995a). Motor development: A new synthesis. *American Psychologist, 50*, 79–95.

Thelen, E. (1995b). Time-scale dynamics and the development of an embodied cognition. In R. Port & T. van Gelder (Eds.), *Mind as motion: Explorations in the dynamics of cognition* (pp. 69–100). Cambridge, MA: MIT Press.

Thornton, I., Pinto, J., & Shiffrar, M. (1998). The visual perception of human locomotion. *Cognitive Neuropsychology, 15*, 535–552.

Tomasello, M., Striano, T., & Rochat, P. (1999). Do young children use objects as symbols? *British Journal of Developmental Psychology, 17*, 563–584.

Trevarthen, C. (1979). Communication and cooperation in infancy: A description of primary intersubjectivity. In M. Bullowa (Ed.), *Before speech: The beginning of interpersonal communication* (pp. 321–347). Cambridge, UK: Cambridge University Press.

Trevarthen, A., & Hubley, P. (1978). Secondary intersubjectivity: Confidence, confiding and acts of meaning in the first year. In A. Locke (Ed.), *Action, gesture and symbol: The emergence of language* (pp. 183–229). London: Academic Press.

Turati, C., Simion, F., Milani, I., & Umilta, C. (2002). Newborns' preference for faces: What is crucial? *Developmental Psychology, 38* (6), 875–882.

Valenza, E., Simion, F., Macchi Cassia, V., & Umilta, C. (1996). Face preference at birth. *Journal of Experimental Psychology: Human Perception and Performance*, **22**, 892–903.

Varela, F., Thompson, E., & Rosch, E. (1991). *The embodied mind: Cognitive science and human experience*. Cambrdige, MA: MIT Press.

Vinter, A. (1986). The role of movement in eliciting early imitations. *Child Development*, **57**, 66–71.

Witt, A., Cermak, S., & Coster, W. (1990). Body part identification in 1- to 2-year-old children. *The American Journal of Occupational Therapy*, **44** (2), 147–153.

Younger, B., & Furrer, S. (2003). A comparison of visual familiarization and object-examining measures of categorization in 9-month-old infants. *Infancy*, **4**, 327–348.

Younger, B., Johnson, K., & Furrer, S. (2004). Infants' comprehension of toy replicas as symbols for real objects. *Cognitive Psychology*, **48**, 207–242.

ACKNOWLEDGMENTS

This work was supported by a University of Queensland Small Research Grant and an Australian Research Council Discovery grant to the first author, and an Australian Postgraduate Award to the second author. This *Monograph* includes data that were collected as part of Michelle Heron's Ph.D. research, and as part of Elizabeth Tilse's Honours research, both at the University of Queensland. We are indebted to a number of scholars for their insightful comments on earlier versions of this manuscript, these include three anonymous reviewers, Rod Ashton, Shaun Gallagher, Ottmar Lipp, John McLean, Derek Moore, Mark Nielsen, Willis Overton, Cathy Reed, Gabrielle Simcock, and Thomas Suddendorf. We also thank James Delaney, Wayne Doran, Emma Lundgren, Kristelle Hudry, Blake McKimmie, Ted McFadden, Luke Smillie, and Melissa Naughton for their advice and/or technical assistance at various stages of the project. Finally, we acknowledge the contribution of the first author's daughter, Rory McFadden, who provided a perfectly illustrative drawing of an impossible human, included as Figure 11.

For correspondence, contact Virginia Slaughter, Early Cognitive Development Unit, School of Psychology, University of Queensland, Brisbane, Australia 4072. E-mail: vps@psy.uq.edu.au.

COMMENTARY

FACING THE BODY: TOWARD A DEVELOPMENTAL THEORY OF BODY KNOWLEDGE

Ulrich Müller and Dana Liebermann

Research on infants' perception of human beings has focused almost entirely on face perception. The face, however, is only one part of the human body and the development of infants' perception and representation of the whole human body has received little attention. For this reason, this *Monograph* co-authored by Slaughter, Heron, Tilse, and Jenkins on the development of infants' representation of the whole human body addresses an important gap in our empirical knowledge. The findings from a number of well-designed experiments reported in this *Monograph* present interesting and valuable data on the development of whole body representations in infancy.

On the basis of neuropsychological research, the authors distinguish between three levels of human body representation: (a) sensori–motor representations of the body, which consist of short-term representations that are responsible for body control and movement; (b) visual–spatial representations of the body, which consist of long-term, general representations involved in the localization of body parts, and (c) lexical–semantic representations of the body involved in the naming of body parts. Whereas sensori–motor representations are considered not to be accessible to consciousness, the other two levels of body knowledge are considered to be accessible.

The research reported in this *Monograph* present a series of eight studies that investigate the development of visual–spatial body representations in 12–24-month-old infants. The key findings that emerge rather consistently across different research methods and materials are that (a) a detailed visual–spatial representation of the human body emerges at around 15- to 18-months, (b) a detailed visual–spatial representation of the human face emerges earlier than a detailed visual–spatial representation of the body, and (c) 12-month-old children fail to categorically discriminate scrambled from nonscrambled human bodies, but are able to discriminate two bodies as well as scrambled and nonscrambled analogues of the human body.

According to the authors, these findings suggest that during the first year of their life, infants have a highly schematic representation of the human body (see also Quinn & Eimas, 1996, 1998, 2000). The activation of these schematic body representations, found in habituation and object examination tasks, results in the failure of 12-months-olds to make a categorical distinction between scrambled and typical bodies. By contrast, because infants do not have schematic representations for body analogues, they process body analogues in more detail and discriminate typical from scrambled body analogues. The developmental course of visual–spatial representations of the human body thus moves from more abstract, schematic representations to more detailed representations.

The findings by Slaughter, Heron, Tilse, and Jenkins raise a number of interesting questions. We will here discuss issues pertinent to (a) the further development of visual–spatial representations of bodies and faces, (b) the modes of processing involved in the representation of bodies, (c) the role of emotion in the processing of bodies, (d) the processes involved in the development of visual–spatial representations, and (e) the broader role of the body in the cognitive development.

The Developmental Course of Visual–Spatial Representations of Faces and Bodies

In the first year of life, infants discriminate scrambled from nonscrambled faces. However, a detailed visual–spatial representation of the human body does not emerge until the middle of the second year. Slaughter and colleagues offer three, not necessarily mutually exclusive, explanations for the finding that visual–spatial representations of faces emerge earlier than visual–spatial representations of human bodies: (a) faces are perceptually easier to learn than bodies; (b) infants have more experience with faces than with bodies; and (c) infants are equipped with an innate schema of human faces.

Interestingly, the performance of older children and adults on face and whole body recognition tasks does not significantly differ, and there is evidence that 3-year-olds perform better on a short-term recognition task that involves whole bodies than on one that involves faces (Seitz, 2002, 2003). Furthermore, 8- and 10-year-old children, as well as adults, perform similarly on face and whole-body recognition when the part–whole paradigm is used (Seitz, 2002). In the part–whole paradigm, whole faces or whole bodies are presented in the encoding phase. In the test phase, pictures of two faces or two bodies are presented in one of two conditions. In the whole-face and the whole-body test conditions, the identical whole face or whole body is presented along with a second face or body in which one feature has been replaced by a new feature (e.g., the familiar mouth has been replaced by new mouth, the familiar hand has been replaced by a new hand). Participants are asked to judge which picture is familiar from the encoding phase. Performance on the whole-face recognition is compared with performance on a part-face and a part-body test condition in which only a pair of isolated features (e.g., only mouth, only hands) is presented. One feature is the same as that presented in the encoding phase, and the other is a new, previously unseen feature. Recognition performance for both children and adults was better when the features were embedded in the context of the whole face or whole body than when the features were presented in isolation (Seitz, 2002). On the basis of these findings, Seitz (2003, p. 126) concludes that face and whole body recognition performance is "similar when the same method is used. However, if differences occur, it is always person recognition that outperforms face recognition." (p. 126)

This conclusion clearly contrasts with the findings reported by Slaughter and colleagues. It is possible that children's face and body representations become more similar as they gain more expertise with human bodies (see also Gauthier, Skudlarski, Gore, & Anderson, 2000). Alternatively, recognition tasks may engage more complex processing than habituation and object examination tasks. Higher-level processing may, as suggested by Slaughter and colleagues, impose similar processing constraints on the representation of faces and bodies, which then results in similar performance on tasks involving faces and bodies. Clearly, additional research is required to chart the developmental course of visual–spatial body representations beyond infancy and to specify the processing constraints imposed by differential levels of task complexity.

Information Processing Involved in Visual–Spatial Representations of the Human Body

The research reported in this *Monograph* presents a first step toward understanding the developmental course of visual–spatial representations of the human body in infancy. Future studies need to examine in more detail the modes by which visual–spatial representations of the human body are processed at different ages, and to compare these modes of processing to those used for faces.

The literature on the representation of faces distinguishes between modes of processing that rely on either feature or configurational information (for a more fine-grained distinction, see Schwaninger, Carbon, & Leder, 2003). Feature information refers to separable features of faces, which are perceived as distinct parts of the face such as the eyes and the mouth (Carey & Diamond, 1977; Schwaninger et al., 2003). Configurational information refers to spatial relations between features such as the distance between the eyes (Bruce, 1988). Infants appear to already use both feature and configurational information already in the first year of life (Cohen & Cashon, 2001; Kestenbaum & Nelson, 1990), although they prefer to process features. Some research studies indicate that between 5 and 7 months of age, infants shift from more feature processing to more configurational processing (Cohen & Cashon, 2001; Schwarzer, Zauner, & Korell, 2003). These changes are generally consistent with Cohen's (1998) information processing approach to development of object perception in infancy, which assumes that infants first process single parts of objects, and later process entire objects as single integrated wholes. However, the availability of both feature and configurational processing modes for faces early in infancy also suggests that face processing differs from object processing (Johnson, 2003).

It is currently unknown which processing mode is used by infants to abstract visual–spatial representations of human bodies, whether the processing of human bodies undergoes similar developmental changes as the processing of faces, and whether the processing of whole bodies is more similar to the processing of faces or to the processing of objects. In the present research, the good performance of 12-months-olds on the abstract human body analogues task (Exp. 5) suggests that insufficient configurational processing skills are not generally responsible for the failure to discriminate scrambled from unscrambled bodies (see also Exps. 2, 4, 6, and 8).

More information about infants' mode of processing human bodies could be generated by using paradigms similar to those used in the study of the representation of faces. The face-inversion paradigm (e.g., Yin, 1969), the switch design (Cohen & Cashon, 2001), and the part-whole paradigm (in the context of a preferential looking paradigm) could provide useful information about how human bodies are processed. For example, the part–whole paradigm provides information about whether processing relies on feature or configurational information (Tanaka, Kay, Grinnell, Stansfield, & Szechter, 1998). If bodies are encoded on the basis of features, then recognition performance should not differ between conditions in which only isolated body parts are presented, and in which whole bodies are presented, because it is the feature that leads to the correct recognition of the body. If bodies are processed more configurationally, then the whole body condition should lead to better performance than the isolated body condition. Older children and adults perform better in the whole-body condition than in the isolated body parts condition, which suggests that they process bodies more configurationally, although there was also some evidence for feature processing, as manifest in the finding that performance in the isolated body parts condition was above chance (Seitz, 2002, 2003). Whether infants use both feature and configurational information in the processing of bodies, whether there are developmental changes in the preferred mode of processing, and how these modes of processing are related to general perceptual development are questions that deserve to be addressed by future research.

Emotions and Body Representation

The human body is more than just a shape: a body individuates a person, is a center of activity, and affords numerous interactions. Infants do not just perceive bodies; they expect other people to reciprocally interact with them (Muir & Nadel, 1998). Early social interactions are dominated by the sharing of affect and emotion, in the context of which infants develop increasingly more complex forms of social understanding. The important function of emotional relatedness in early social interactions is succinctly expressed by Hobson's (2002, p. 59) statement that "it is through emotional relatedness that a baby discovers what kind of thing a person is." In the light of the important role of emotional relatedness in early infancy, infants' visual–spatial representations of human bodies may develop out of dynamic and emotionally charged embodied interactions. Furthermore, infants might be capable of distinguishing different emotions that are displayed in movements before they are capable of forming detailed visual–spatial representations of the human body. To examine this possibility, point-light displays of human movements that express different emotions could be used with infants.

Along with picking up the emotions expressed by a body, infants' very perception of other bodies may be imbued with affect. For example, Heinz Werner (1930) suggests that in primordial perception things have an emotional-expressive and dynamic tone; they "speak" to us. Werner refers to this primordial form of perception as physiognomic perception. Physiognomic perception is rooted in vital, bodily, affective-motor feelings, and it forms the basis for the development of more analytical forms of perception.

Recent neuropsychological findings of patients with Capgras delusion lend support to the idea that emotional arousal plays an important role in face recognition. Capgras delusion, believed to result from damage to the ventral processing route, refers to the belief that significant others (friends, family members) have been replaced by impostors (Ellis & Lewis, 2001). Perplexingly, patients with Capgras delusion seem on one level to recognize a face but at the same time deny its authenticity. Research has shown that patients with Capgras delusion do not display covert face recognition (i.e., differential autonomic arousal to familiar faces, as measured by skin conductance responses). Thus, patients with Capgras delusion appear to have an intact overt face recognition system but an impaired covert face recognition system, which is exactly opposite to the pattern displayed by patients with prosopagnosia. In order to account for intact overt recognition in the absence of covert recognition, a dual route model of face recognition has been suggested (Ellis & Lewis, 2001). According to this model, face recognition occurs along to independent routes, a dorsal route extracting identity information, and a ventral route extracting the emotional significance of faces. To explore the contribution of emotional arousal to the recognition of bodies, infants and children's physiological reactions to familiar and unfamiliar bodies could be examined.

Processes Involved in the Development of Visual–Spatial Representation

Slaughter and colleagues discuss three possible origins of schematic visual–spatial representations: Schematic visual–spatial representations are (a) innate, (b) learned through perceptual analyses (Mandler, 1998), and (c) derived from sensori–motor representations. They attribute the latter position to Piaget and suggest that representational redescription (Karmiloff-Smith, 1992) is the process that transforms sensori–motor representations into visual–spatial representations of the body.

Imitation is another process that could lead to the development of detailed visual–spatial representations of the human body. Piaget, in fact, does not derive the visual–spatial representation of the whole body from sensori–motor representations. He holds that sensori–motor coordinations generate knowledge about individual parts of the body (e.g., hands, feet), but sensori–motor coordinations do not provide knowledge of the whole body (Piaget, 1960). Instead, he believes that imitation is the figurative instrument that generates a detailed visual–spatial representation of one's own body and the bodies of other people. Further, Piaget (1960) proposes that spatial operations are required to establish correct spatial relations between the individual parts that enter the body representation complex. Although this aspect is not further explicated in his writings, it is likely that he considers the progress made in the construction of a more complex practical concept of space relevant here (Piaget, 1954).

At the end of the first year of life, infants begin to imitate new movements and attempt to reproduce the movements that lead to an interesting effect (instead of being focused on reproducing the effect; see Guillaume, 1971; Meltzoff, 1988; Piaget, 1962). There are two reasons for supposing that these new imitative skills may contribute to the development of a detailed visual–spatial representation of the body. First, through these imitative behaviors infants establish a correspondence between the internal kinesthetic perceptions (the lived body) and the external representation of the body, which results in the objectification of the body. Second, these imitative behaviors require that the infant perceptually analyzes the behavior of the model and compares her actions with those of the model, which heightens awareness of her and the model's body. Future research could test the proposal that imitation contributes to the development of more visual–spatial representations of the human body by examining the predictive relations between imitative skills and performance on categorical body discrimination tasks.

Embodiment

The visual–spatial representation of human bodies is only one aspect of embodiment. According to the embodiment position, different aspects of psychological functioning are grounded in bodily experience (Overton, 1994). This idea is nicely expressed by Thelen (2000, p. 5): "To say that cognition is embodied means that it arises from bodily interactions with the world and is continually meshed with them. From this point of view, therefore, cognition depends on the kinds of experiences that come from having a body with a particular perceptual and motor capabilities that are inseparably linked and that together form the matrix within which reasoning, memory, emotion, language, and all other aspects of mental life are embedded." The specific form of human embodiment, however, raises interesting questions, which yet have to be addressed in developmental psychology.

The most comprehensive theory of embodiment was developed by the French philosopher Maurice Merleau-Ponty. According to Merleau-Ponty (1962), our consciousness is situated in the world by means of the lived body. Our body is not inaccessible to consciousness; rather, consciousness is intentionally directed toward things through the intermediary of the body (Merleau-Ponty, 1962, p. 138). Moreover, in a significant sense, the lived body helps to constitute this world-as-experienced. We cannot understand the meaning and form of objects without reference to the bodily powers through which we engage them—our senses, motility, language, desires. The lived body is not just one thing in the world but a way in which the world, as we experience it, comes to be.

The lived body must be contrasted with another form of experiencing the body. Although consciousness cannot be conceived except as embodied (I am my body), in another sense there are times when we can identify consciousness as distinct from, although still related to, the body (I have a body). For example, we distinguish between mind and physical body when we are or our body poses an obstacle to our projects. The body has an ambiguous role for a human being: it is experienced from within and can be experienced from without, as a physical thing.

This ambiguous role of the body has been captured by Plessner's (1928, pp. 288–346) term "eccentric position." The term implies that for human beings the body has a double role: a "human being always and conjointly is a living body (head, trunk, extremities, with all that these contain) . . . and has this living body as this physical thing" (Plessner, 1970, p. 35). The lived body is experienced from within and constitutes the absolute focal point of reference of all things in the environment. By contrast, to understand the body as a physical thing, the absolute focal point of reference must be left and the lived body (including consciousness) must be localized relative to and on the same plane as other things (Plessner, 1970, 1983). Crucial to the understanding of the body as a physical thing is the ability to objectify the body from the outside. This ability is closely related to the ability to take an instrumental attitude toward one's body: although animals live the instrumentality of their body but are not aware of having an instrumental relation to their body, human beings are aware of this instrumental relation, and their body becomes the instrument on which they play (Plessner, 1983, p. 319).

By distinguishing between the lived body and the body as a physical thing human beings not only have an inner life as distinct from their physical existence; they, in addition, "stand over and against both of these, holding them apart from one another and yet together" (Grene, 1974, p. 341). As a consequence, a human being can experience himself the center of his inner life, as being enclosed by the lived body into which he is stuck as if in a case (Plessner, 1983, p. 178).

The body as lived body and as a physical thing are thus intertwined, and human beings live this dual relationship: "I go walking with my consciousness, my body is its bearer, on whose momentary position the selective content and perspective of my consciousness depend; and I go walking in my consciousness, and my body with its changes of position appears as the content of its sphere" (Plessner, 1970, p. 36).

The dual role of the body as lived body and physical thing raises interesting questions for developmental psychologists: When do children start to objectify their body? Are their different levels of objectification? What are the processes that lead to the objectification of the body? How do children negotiate the ambiguity of the body at different levels of development?

Some clues about the developmental course of the objectification of the body can be gathered from Piaget's observations on infants' development of the practical concept of space. For example, when Piaget's daughter Jacqueline was 16 months old, she tried to grasp a piece of cloth while she was standing on top of it (Piaget, 1963, Obs. 168). This behavior demonstrates that Jacqueline was not yet capable of completely objectifying her body because she did not locate her body within the same space as other objects. Other clues about the development of the objectification of the body can be gathered from mirror self-recognition (Brooks-Gunn, & Lewis, 1984). In order to recognize herself in the mirror, the infant must relate her proprioceptive, lived body to the external, visually displayed body in the mirror (Brooks-Gunn, & Lewis, 1984; Mitchell, 1997). It is likely that the objectification of the body is a prerequisite for the emergence of lexical–semantic body representations of the body, and that it promotes new ways of using the body as a means of expression. Clearly, the developmental course of the objectification of the body, as well as possible ramifications of this process on how the human body is perceived and represented deserves more empirical attention.

Conclusion

The findings reported in this *Monograph* reveal clear age-related changes in the development of visual–spatial representation of the human body in infancy. These data specify the direction of the development of visual–spatial representation of the human body as well as constrain speculations about processes underlying this development. As we have argued, the findings also leave many important questions unanswered, including the extended course of the developmental trajectory, the type of information processing involved in the perception of human bodies, the role of emotions in the perception of human bodies, as well as larger issues surrounding the concept of embodiment. Future studies on the development of body knowledge should focus on age-related changes in the information processing underlying body representations, as well as on the processes that lead from global to more detailed visual–spatial representations of the human body, and eventually result in lexical–semantic representations of the human body. Such research will yield richer information about the overall development of body knowledge in terms of the three levels of human body representation defined by Slaughter, Heron, Tilse, and Jenkins. Undoubtedly, this *Monograph* will stimulate future theorizing and empirical research, which, in turn, will continue to make us face the body.

References

Brooks-Gunn, J., & Lewis, M. (1984). The development of early visual self-recognition. *Developmental Review*, **4**, 215–239.

Bruce, V. (1988). *Recognizing faces*. Hillsdale, NJ: Lawrence Erlbaum.

Carey, S., & Diamond, R. (1977). From piecemeal to configurational representation of faces. *Science*, **195**, 312–314.

Cohen, L. B. (1998). An information-processing approach to infant perception and cognition. In F. Simion & G. Butterworth (Eds.), *The development of sensory, motor, and cognitive capacities in early infancy* (pp. 277–300). Hove, UK: Psychology Press.

Cohen, L. B., & Cashon, C. H. (2001). Do 7-month-old infants process independent features or facial configurations? *Infant & Child Development*, **10**, 83–92.

Ellis, H. D., & Lewis, M. B. (2001). Capgras delusion: A window on face recognition. *Trends in Cognitive Sciences*, **5**, 149–156.

Gauthier, I., Skudlarski, P., Gore, J. C., & Anderson, A. W. (2000). Expertise for cars and birds recruits brain areas involved in face recognition. *Nature Neuroscience*, **3**, 191–197.

Grene, M. (1974). The characters of living things. III: Helmuth Plessner's theory of organic modals. In M. Grene (Ed.), *The understanding of nature* (pp. 320–345). Dordrecht: D. Reidel Publishing Company.

Guillaume, P. (1971). *Imitation in children.* Chicago: University of Chicago Press. (Original work published in 1926.)

Hobson, P. (2002). *The cradle of thought: Exploring the origins of thinking.* London: Macmillan.

Johnson, S. P. (2003). Development of fragmented versus holistic object perception. In G. Schwarzer & H. Leder (Eds.), *The development of face processing* (pp. 3–17). Göttingen: Hogrefe & Huber.

Karmiloff-Smith, A. (1992). *Beyond modularity: A developmental perspective on cognitive science.* Cambridge, MA: MIT Press.

Kestenbaum, R., & Nelson, C. A. (1990). The recognition and categorization of upright and inverted emotional expressions by 7-month-old infants. *Infant Behavior & Development*, **13**, 497–511.

Mandler, J. (1998). Representation. In D. Kuhn & R. Siegler (Vol. Eds.) & W. Damon (Series Ed.), *Handbook of child psychology, Vol. 2: Cognition, perception and language* (pp. 255–308). New York: Wiley.

Meltzoff, A. N. (1988). Infant imitation after a 1-week delay: Long-term memory for novel acts and multiple stimuli. *Developmental Psychology*, **24**, 470–476.

Merleau-Ponty, M. (1962). *The phenomenology of perception.* New York: Humanities Press. (Original work published in 1945)

Mitchell, R. W. (1997). Kinesthetic–visual matching and the self-concept as explanations of mirror self-recognition. *Journal for the Theory of Social Behavior*, **27**, 17–39.

Muir, D. W., & Nadel, J. (1998). Infant social perception. In A. Slater (Ed.), *Perceptual development: Visual, auditory, and speech perception in infancy* (pp. 247–285). Hove: Psychology Press.

Overton, W. (1994). Contexts of meaning: The computational and the embodied mind. In W. F. Overton & D. S. Palermo (Eds.), *The nature and ontogenesis of meaning* (pp. 1–18). Hillsdale, NJ: Lawrence Erlbaum.

Piaget, J. (1954). *The construction of reality in the child.* New York: Basic Books. (Original work published 1937.)

Piaget, J. (1960). Les praxies chez l'enfant. *Revue Neurologique*, **102**, 551–565.

Piaget, J. (1962). *Play, dreams, and imitation.* New York: Norton. (Original work published 1945.)

Piaget, J. (1963). *The origins of intelligence in children.* New York: W. W. Norton & Company, Inc. (Original work published in 1936.)

Plessner, H. (1928). *Die Stufen des Organischen und der Mensch [The levels of the organic and the human being].* Berlin: Göschen.

Plessner, H. (1970). *Laughing and crying: A study of the limits of human behavior.* (J. S. Churchill & M. Grene, Trans.). Evanston, IL: Northwestern University Press. (Original work published in 1941.)

Plessner, H. (1983). *Gesammelte Schriften, Vol. 8.* Frankfurt: Suhrkamp.

Quinn, P. C., & Eimas, P. D. (1996). Perceptual cues permit categorical differentiation of animal species by infants. *Journal of Experimental Child Psychology*, **63**, 189–211.

Quinn, P. C., & Eimas, P. D. (1998). Evidence for a global categorical representation of humans by young infants. *Journal of Experimental Child Psychology*, **69**, 151–174.

Quinn, P. C., & Eimas, P. D. (2000). The emergence of category representations during infancy: Are separate and conceptual processes required? *Journal of Cognition & Development*, **1**, 55–61.

Schwaninger, A., Carbon, C. C., & Leder, H. (2003). Expert face processing: Specialization and constraints. In G. Schwarzer & H. Leder (Eds.), *Development of face processing* (pp. 81–97). Göttingen: Hogrefe & Huber.

Schwarzer, G., Zauner, N., & Korrell, M. (2003). Face processing during the first decade of life. In G. Schwarzer & H. Leder (Eds.), *Development of face processing* (pp. 55–68). Göttingen: Hogrefe & Huber.

Seitz, K. (2002). Parts and wholes in person recognition: Developmental trends. *Journal of Experimental Child Psychology*, **82**, 367–381.

Seitz, K. (2003). Face processing and person processing: Are they both the same? In G. Schwarzer & H. Leder (Eds.), *The development of face processing* (pp. 121–135). Göttingen: Hogrefe & Huber.

Tanaka, J. W., Kay, J. B., Grinnell, E., Stansfield, B., & Szechter, L. (1998). Face recognition in young children: When the whole is greater than the sum of its parts. *Visual Cognition*, **5**, 479–496.

Thelen, E. (2000). Grounded in the world: Developmental origins of the embodied mind. *Infancy*, **1**, 3–28.

Werner, H. (1930). Untersuchungen über Empfinden I: Das Problem des Empfindens und das Problem seiner experimentellen Prüfung. *Zeitschrift für Psychologie*, **114**, 152–166.

Yin, R. K. (1969). Looking at upside-down faces. *Journal of Experimental Psychology*, **81**, 141–145.

CONTRIBUTORS

Virginia Slaughter (Ph.D., 1994, University of California at Berkeley) is a developmental psychologist specializing in social-cognitive development. Her research interests center around the question of how infants and young children conceptualize human beings. She is currently Associate Editor for the *Australian Journal of Psychology* and for the *British Journal of Developmental Psychology*. She has been at the University of Queensland since 1996, where she is a Senior Lecturer and Co-director of the Early Cognitive Development Unit in the School of Psychology.

Michelle Heron (B.A. (Hons I) 2000, University of Queensland) is a Ph.D. student and part-time lecturer at University of Queensland, Australia. Her research interests include infants' knowledge of the human body shape and infants' understanding of the relation between representations and their referents.

Elizabeth Tilse (B.Sc. (Hons) 2001, University of Queensland) is currently employed as a research officer in the Department of Psychiatry and the School of Social Work and Applied Human Sciences at the University of Queensland.

Linda Jenkins (B.A. 2000, University of Queensland) is currently a part-time Honours student in Psychology, as well as Lab Manager of the Early Cognitive Development Unit in the School of Psychology at the University of Queensland.

Ulrich Müller (Ph.D., 1998, Temple University) is Assistant Professor at the University of Victoria, British Columbia. His research centers on the early development of social understanding, executive function, and reasoning. He serves on the Editorial Boards of *Child Development*, and the *Journal of*

Cognition and Development, and is a member of the Board of Directors of the Jean Piaget Society.

Dana Liebermann (Honors B.Sc., 2002, University of Toronto) is a graduate student in life-span developmental psychology at the University of Victoria, British Columbia. Her research centers on the development of executive functioning and reasoning in preschool children.

STATEMENT OF EDITORIAL POLICY

The *Monographs* series is devoted to publishing developmental research that generates authoritative new findings and uses these to foster fresh, better integrated, or more coherent perspectives on major developmental issues, problems, and controversies. The significance of the work in extending developmental theory and contributing definitive empirical information in support of a major conceptual advance is the most critical editorial consideration. Along with advancing knowledge on specialized topics, the series aims to enhance cross-fertilization among developmental disciplines and developmental sub fields. Therefore, clarity of the links between the specific issues under study and questions relating to general developmental processes is important. These links, as well as the manuscript as a whole, must be as clear to the general reader as to the specialist. The selection of manuscripts for editorial consideration, and the shaping of manuscripts through reviews-and-revisions, are processes dedicated to actualizing these ideals as closely as possible.

Typically *Monographs* entail programmatic large-scale investigations; sets of programmatic interlocking studies; or—in some cases—smaller studies with highly definitive and theoretically significant empirical findings. Multi-authored sets of studies that center on the same underlying question can also be appropriate; a critical requirement here is that all studies address common issues, and that the contribution arising from the set as a whole be unique, substantial, and well integrated. The needs of integration preclude having individual chapters identified by individual authors. In general, irrespective of how it may be framed, any work that is judged to significantly extend developmental thinking will be taken under editorial consideration.

To be considered, submissions should meet the editorial goals of *Monographs* and should be no briefer than a minimum of 80 pages (including references and tables). There is an upper limit of 175–200 pages. In exceptional circumstances this upper limit may be modified. (Please submit four copies.) Because a *Monograph* is inevitable lengthy and usually substantively complex, it is particularly important that the text be well organized and written in clear, precise, and literate English. Note, however, that authors from non-English-speaking countries should not be put off by this stricture. In accordance with the general aims of SRCD, this series is actively interested in promoting international exchange of developmental research. Neither membership in the Society nor affiliation with the academic discipline of psychology are relevant in considering a *Monographs* submission.

The corresponding author for any manuscript must, in the submission letter, warrant that all coauthors are in agreement with the content of the manuscript. The corresponding author also is responsible for informing all coauthors, in a timely manner, of manuscript submission, editorial decisions, reviews received, and any revisions recommended. Before publication, the corresponding author also must warrant in the submission letter that the study has been conducted according to the ethical guidelines of the Society for Research in Child Development.

Potential authors who may be unsure whether the manuscript they are planning would make an appropriate submission are invited to draft an outline of what they propose, and send it to the Editor for assessment. This mechanism, as well as a more detailed description of all editorial policies, evaluation process, and format requirements can be found at the Editorial Office web site (http://astro.temple.edu/~overton/monosrcd.html) or by contacting the Editor, Wills F. Overton, Temple University-Psychology, 1701 North 13th St. – Rm 567, Philadelphia, PA 19122-6085 (e-mail: monosrcd@temple.edu) (telephone: 1-215-204-7360).

Monographs of the Society for Research in Child Development (ISSN 0037-976X), one of two publications of Society of Research in Child Development, is published three times a year by Blackwell Publishing, Inc., with offices at 350 Main Street, Malden, MA 02148, USA, and 9600 Garsington Road, Oxford OX4 2XG, UK. Call US (800) 835-6770 or (781) 388-8206, UK +44 (0) 1865 778315; fax US (781) 388-8232, UK +44 (0) 1865 471775; e-mail US subscrip@bos.blackwellpublishing.com, UK customerservices@oxon.blackwellpublishing.com. A subscription to *Monographs of the SRCD* comes with a subscription to *Child Development* (published bimonthly).

INFORMATION FOR SUBSCRIBERS   For new orders, renewals, sample copy requests, claims, change of address, and all other subscription correspondence, please contact the Journals Subscription Department at your nearest Blackwell office.

INSTITUTIONAL PREMIUM RATES* FOR MONOGRAPHS OF THE SRCD/CHILD DEVELOPMENT 2004   The Americas $420, Rest of World £298. Customers in Canada should add 7% GST to The Americas price or provide evidence of entitlement to exemption. Customers in the UK and EU should add VAT at 5% or provide a VAT registration number or evidence of entitlement to exemption.

*Includes print plus premium online access to the current and all available backfiles. Print and online-only rates are also available. For more information about Blackwell Publishing journals, including online access information, terms and conditions, and other pricing options, please visit www.blackwellpublishing.com or contact our customer service department, tel: (800) 835-6770 or (781) 388-8206 (US office); +44 (0)1865 778315 (UK office).

BACK ISSUES   Back issues are available from the publisher at the current single issue rate.

MICROFORM   The journal is available on microfilm. For microfilm service, address inquiries to ProQuest Information and Learning, 300 North Zeeb Road, Ann Arbor, MI 48106-1346, USA. Bell and Howell Serials Customer Service Department: (800) 521-0600 × 2873.

ADVERTISING   For information and rates, please visit the journal's website at www.blackwellpublishing.com/MONO email: blackwellads@aidcvt.com, or contact Faith Elliott, Blackwell Advertising Representative, 50 Winter Sport Lane, PO Box 80, Williston, VT 05495. Phone: 800-866-1684 or Fax: 802-864-7749.

MAILING   Journal is mailed Standard Rate. Mailing to rest of world by Deutsche Post Global Mail. Canadian mail is sent by Canadian publications mail agreement number 40573520. Postmaster: Send all address changes to Monographs of the Societey for Research in Child Development, Blackwell Publishing Inc., Journals Subscription Department, 350 Main St., Malden, MA 02148-5018.

Blackwell Synergy   Sign up to receive Blackwell *Synergy* free e-mail alerts with complete *Monographs of the SRCD* tables of contents and quick links to article abstracts from the most current issue. Simply go to www.blackwell-synergy.com, select the journal from the list of journals, and click on "Sign-up" for FREE email table of contents alerts.